BIBLE

G000130925

BIBLE CLASS COMMENTARY

GALATIANS · EPHESIANS
PHILIPPIANS · COLOSSIANS

Henry T. Mahan

 EVANGELICAL PRESS

EVANGELICAL PRESS
12 Wooler Street, Darlington, Co. Durham, DL1 1RQ,
England

© Evangelical Press 1985

First published 1985
Reprinted 1991

ISBN 0 85234 210 1

Cover picture by kind permission of Rev. R. Simpson.

Typset in Great Britain by Beaver ReproGraphics, Ware.
Printed by Courier International Ltd.

Contents

Galatians

On mixing grace and works

Galatians 1:1-10

Paul had planted several churches in Galatia and was now a prisoner at Rome. Some false teachers had seduced some of these Galatians from the gospel of free grace preached by Paul, persuading them that observance of the Levitical ceremonies was necessary to salvation and that justification before God was partly through faith in Christ and partly from their own works. They also said that Paul was not really an apostle like the other apostles who had been with Christ during his earthly ministry and, therefore, Paul's doctrine was not to be accepted. Paul wrote to convince the Galatians of their error, to turn them back to Christ alone and to press upon them the duties of a holy life.

v.1. Paul claims to be an apostle, the highest office in the church. He did not receive this office from a group of men, or from any one man, but from the Lord Jesus Christ and from God the Father (Acts 26:13-18). His office was confirmed by signs and miracles. Christ appeared to him, Christ was seen by him and he received his gospel from Christ (Gal. 1:11,12).

v.2. This letter and greeting are not only from Paul but from all of the brethren who were with Paul and who assisted him in the ministry. The letter is to all of the churches of Galatia. The churches were not national but congregational; each local assembly was autonomous, functioning independently without control by the others.

v.3. Paul wishes for them *the gracious favour* and *goodwill* of God, whereby he is pleased with his elect in Christ (Eph. 1:3-7), and *peace* with God — peace of conscience, peace with one another and even peace with their enemies. God is the fountain of peace and grace, and Christ is the means to convey grace and peace to us.

v.4.   Having mentioned the Lord Jesus in verse 3, Paul goes on to describe our Redeemer by his one great act as the great High Priest over the house of God, by which he redeemed, justified, sanctified and delivered us from guilt, wrath and condemnation from this present evil world. He gave himself, soul and body, for our sins on the cross of Calvary (Heb. 9:26; 10:12-14).

v.5.   Here is the duty and occupation of the saved — to ascribe all glory and praise to the Father, Son and Holy Spirit. The glory of Christ and our gratitude to him are the theme of our lives and shall be the long-lasting and never-ending song of the redeemed throughout eternity (Rev. 5:13).

R + R

vv.6, 7.   Paul enters into the subject matter of this epistle, which is to reprove and rebuke any man who leaves the gospel of God's free grace and attempts to mix works with grace (Rom. 11:5,6). It is surprising and astonishing that any person who has heard the good news of salvation by the grace of God through the merits of Christ would leave that gospel and look to a perverted gospel of grace plus works. But that is what these Galatians were doing. These teachers had persuaded the people to leave Paul's message and receive theirs, which added circumcision, ceremonies, holy days and human works to the works of Christ. This is not a gospel (good news) at all but a perverted system of self-righteousness (1 Cor. 1:30; Col. 1:19-22; 2:8-15).

vv.8, 9.   The apostle then expressed the seriousness of their error. 'If any person preaches any other way of salvation except the full, sufficient, complete and eternal redemption that Jesus Christ by himself accomplished on behalf of his elect (which requires nothing of the creature but faith), even if it be an angel from heaven, let that person be accursed.' Paul also says, 'If *we* bring any other gospel, let *us* be accursed.' He repeats the warning for emphasis.

v.10. 'Are we trying to win the favour of man or of God?
Do we seek to be men-pleasers? If we are seeking the favour
and approval of men, we are not the bond-servants of Jesus
Christ. Our aim is to be true to the Word of God, and in doing
so we will be true to our hearers.' This gospel of the free grace
of God is glorifying to God and honouring to all of his excellent attributes — his love and mercy, his infinite wisdom, his
righteous justice and his immutable holiness. This gospel of the
free grace of God in Christ is the only hope that sinful, corrupt
men have; for if righteousness comes by any obedience to the
law at all, not only did Christ die in vain, but no son of Adam
has any hope of being saved.

Paul - the apostle

Galatians 1:11-24

The false prophets, who had seduced the churches of Galatia
from the gospel of free grace and persuaded them that the
observance of the Levitical ceremonies (fulfilled and abolished
by Christ) was necessary for salvation and that justification
and salvation were partly from faith in Christ and partly from
their own works, had also charged that Paul was not a true
apostle and that his doctrine was a fake. This is what Paul is
dealing with in these verses. We are certainly in trouble if Paul
is not an apostle, for he is responsible for about one half of the
New Testament which we read and believe.

v.11. These false teachers did not say that the gospel was
man-made nor that it came from men (for they themselves
pretended to preach the gospel), but they argued that Paul had
no authority for what he preached other than human authority
and thus was not to be followed. Therefore, Paul says that the
gospel of free grace in Christ alone (which he preached) is **'not
from man'**, nor is he an ordinary preacher, but an appointed
apostle of Christ.

v.12.   You and I do receive the gospel from men, and we are
taught by men. It is true that the Holy Spirit opens our hearts,
enlightens our minds and reveals the gospel to us; but he uses
human teachers, preachers and witnesses. This is why we
should search the Word, try the spirits and take heed what we
hear! But an apostle (like Paul) did not receive the gospel this
way; he learned it by revelation from Jesus Christ. That is why
we can quote the apostle and be sure that we are quoting and
following God (2 Tim. 3:16; 2 Peter 1:20,21).

vv.13,14.   'I am no stranger to the Levitical law and ceremonies,' he says. The works, deeds and circumcision which the
false teachers wished to add to the gospel and required of
them were at one time his only hope for salvation and his only
message.   *but not now!*
     1. Paul was born of Jewish parents, had a Jewish education,
followed the Jewish law to the letter and lived as a Pharisee
(Acts 26:4,5; Phil. 3:5,6).
     2. He hated Jesus Christ and persecuted the church. Sal-
vation by grace (apart from human merit) was a gospel which
he tried to destroy.
     3. His ability to defend the law was above and beyond that
of many who were his equal in age. He was the champion and
leader (both in ability and zeal) of those who defended the
traditions and laws of his fathers. In other words, these works-
and-law advocates were not dealing with a novice. Paul ex-
ceeded them all in every way as an advocate of salvation by
works.

v.15.   Here Paul begins to relate his conversion — his call, the
revelation of Christ in his heart and the direct revelation of the
gospel to him by the Master.
     1. God chose Paul to salvation and to the apostleship before
he was born, yes, before the foundation of the world, as God
has chosen all of his people (Jer. 1:5; Eph. 1:3,4; 2 Thess.
2:13).
     2. When it pleased God (in God's own time), he stopped
Paul on his road of rebellion, enlightened him and called him
to Christ (Rom. 8:29,30; 2 Tim. 1:9; John 6:37,44,45).

v.16. Christ was revealed *to* Paul as the Messiah, the atonement, the sin-offering, the fulfilment of every type, prophecy
and ceremony, and in the glory of his person and work. But
Christ was revealed *in* Paul, for Christ was formed in him.
Christ's Spirit dwelt in him, Christ's grace was implanted in
him and now he lived by the faith of the Son of God. Paul
needed no ceremony, circumcision, nor works to make him
complete; he was complete in Christ (1 Cor. 1:30). After this
revelation of Christ in Paul, he did not confer with other men
to verify it or complete it.

v.17. 'I did not seek out those who were apostles before I
was called to be an apostle, but I went to Arabia; afterwards I
came back to Damascus.' What he did there, how long he
stayed and what ministry he pursued we are not told anywhere.

vv.18,19. 'After three years I visited the apostle Peter and
spent fifteen days with him. I did not talk to any of the other
apostles except James.' This is observed to show that Paul did
not receive his gospel from men, even from the other apostles
of Christ. His sole authority and revelation came from Christ.

vv.20-24. 'What I have written to you is the truth. I did not
receive my gospel from the apostles nor from the churches of
Judea. I did not visit them and was unknown to them except
by reputation. They heard of me, rejoiced and praised God
that he was pleased to save me and call me to preach Christ.'

Confirming the gospel of grace

Galatians 2:1-13

As we approach this chapter, we must keep in mind the grand
points that Paul establishes in this epistle:
  1. Justification is by faith in Christ alone apart from works,
the Levitical law, or religious ceremony.

2. Paul is truly an apostle as much as Peter, James or John.

3. He is a chosen vessel to bear the gospel of Christ to the Gentiles.

Cancel at J.

v.1.   This is the trip (mentioned in Acts 15:1,2) which Paul made to Jerusalem with Barnabas, concerning the question of whether circumcision is necessary to salvation. Titus, who was a Greek and a minister of the gospel, went with him. Titus was an uncircumcised Gentile, a living testimony of the apostle's message and practice.

v.2.   They did not send for him, nor did he go to Jerusalem by a vote of the church. He felt led of God to go and talk privately with those who were apostles before him, men of great esteem and reputation. The issue was the theme of this epistle — that salvation is wholly by grace and does not require the keeping of the ceremonial law. If salvation were by anything but grace, Paul's ministry was all in vain.

v.3.   There was such agreement between Paul and the other apostles regarding the matter of the law and circumcision that Titus, an uncircumcised Greek, was accepted as a brother and fellow minister on the spot. They required nothing further of him. If these ceremonies were necessary, the apostles of Christ would have required them of Titus!

vv.4,5.   This is why Paul and the apostles refused to circumcise Titus. If it had been a thing indifferent and only to satisfy some weak believers (as in the case of Timothy, Acts 16:1-3), he would have complied. The false prophets who had crept in insisted that circumcision and other ceremonies were necessary to salvation. Paul would not give in to such error for an hour!

v.6.   These other apostles were reputed to be great, and they were (though their office and position made no difference to Paul, for his gospel was given him by God; besides, the Lord is not impressed with men's persons or position). These men imposed no new requirements on Paul, added nothing to his gospel and made no suggestions.

vv. 7, 8.   'But on the contrary, when they saw that I was ordained of God to carry the gospel to the Gentiles just as definitely as Peter was ordained to carry the gospel to the Jews, they were agreeable and rejoiced. For God, who motivated and equipped Peter for his work among the Jews, also prepared me to preach to the Gentiles' (Acts 9:13-15).

vv. 9, 10.   James, Peter and John, who seemed to be the spokesmen and pillars of the church, gave Paul and Barnabas their blessings and approval of the ministry to the Gentiles and made only one stipulation — that they remember and minister to the poor, which they were eager to do!

vv. 11-13.   Evidently this incident occurred between Paul and the other apostles after the meeting in Jerusalem and it shows us several things.

1. How deeply ingrained the ceremonial law, circumcision and Jewish pride were in these Jews.

2. How the best of men (even apostles) are still men and subject to fall and error.

3. How Satan hates the gospel of pure grace and will use choice men to cause division.

4. How we ought to stand firm for salvation by grace through faith even when it means rebuking a leader or a close friend.

Peter had agreed with Paul's gospel and given his blessings to his ministry. But when these Jews came down from Jerusalem to Antioch, Peter feared their disfavour and withdrew from the Gentiles. Having much influence, he caused a strong division among the brethren, even causing Barnabas (who knew better) to take part in his hypocrisy. We shall take up Paul's word to Peter in the next section.

weakness of Peter

Justified by Christ alone

Galatians 2:14-21

When Paul, Barnabas and Titus met with the apostles in
Jerusalem, Peter was there. Titus, being a Greek believer, was
not compelled to be circumcised according to the Jewish law
and Peter agreed with the others that circumcision was of the
heart and not the flesh. When the apostles gave their right
hands of fellowship and blessings to Paul and Barnabas to go
to the Gentiles with the gospel of free grace in Christ apart
from works, laws and ceremonies, Peter also gave his blessings.
And when Peter came to Antioch to visit, he ate and fellow-
shipped with the Gentile believers without reservation. But
when some of the Jewish brethren who were prominent Jews
and zealous of the law came to Antioch, Peter, fearing their
disfavour and criticism, withdrew from the Gentiles, causing a
division among the brethren to the point of influencing even
Barnabas to avoid the uncircumcised Gentiles. Paul rebuked
Peter, Barnabas and these zealous Jews. His remarks were
directed especially to Peter.

v.14.   Their walk was not in integrity, sincerity and truth,
because previously they had agreed that there was no joining
of ceremony and grace nor of Moses and Christ. Their walk
certainly was contrary to the gospel of Christ; so Paul said,
'Peter, if you, who were born, brought up and obliged to
observe all of the Levitical law, no longer feel in bondage to
these ceremonies and laws (you know in your heart you are
free from this yoke; all righteousness is fulfilled in Christ),
why do you compel these Gentiles to live under these laws?'

v.15.   Since the apostles (who were born Jews and therefore
under the law of Moses and under obligation to keep it until
Christ came) had now relinquished the law of Moses and

wholly believed in Christ for all righteousness and acceptance
with God, then it was totally unreasonable to lead Gentiles,
who were never under the Levitical law, to observe it!

v.16.   We know that a man is not justified by the law.

1. We know this from the law itself, which requires perfect
obedience (Gal. 3:10; 4:21).

2. We know this from the gospel, which clearly states that
we are complete in Christ (1 Cor. 1:30; Col. 2:9,10).

3. We know this from experience, being fully convinced of
the insufficiency of human righteousness (Rom. 7:18).

4. We know that we are justified by that faith which has
Christ as its author, finisher and object.

We are justified by God of his own will through the merits
and blood of Christ. Faith believes Christ, receives Christ and
lays hold upon Christ and his righteousness. It is called the
faith of Christ because he is the author of it as well as the
object of it.

vv.17,18.   'If we seek to be justified by Christ and do not
rest in him alone (in his righteousness, his obedience, his blood
and his intercession) but seek to add to Christ our own works,
righteousness and obedience to the ceremonies of the law,
then Christ, instead of being a minister of a perfect righteousness and acceptance, becomes a minister of the law (which is
the strength of sin, 1 Cor. 15:56) and the minister of condemnation and death. Is this the work and ministry of Christ?
God forbid!

If I restore the ceremonies of the law (such as circumcision,
holy days, foods and drinks — the things which I preach as
fulfilled by Christ, through Christ and in Christ), then I make
myself an unjustified sinner. I could not be otherwise, for the
law demands perfection, and if, in Christ, I am not perfected,
then I am a transgressor.'

v.19.   **'For I, through the law** of Christ (the doctrine of grace
or the gospel of free grace) which says, "Believe on the Lord
Jesus Christ and thou shalt be saved" (all of our pardon,
righteousness, acceptance and life comes through Christ), **am**

dead to the law which says, "Do this or that and thou shalt
live." **"That I might live unto God**," not in sin, nor in violation
of his moral law, nor in neglect of holiness and integrity, but
that I should live in the will of God for his honour and glory.'
Believers who are not under law but under grace do not desire
to live in sin but consider themselves under a greater law — the
law of his love.

v.20.   **'I am crucified with Christ**. He bore my sins in his
body on the tree and destroyed and made an end to them.
They have no damning nor condemning power (Rom. 8:1,
33,34). The world is crucified unto me and I unto the world.
My desire is to walk with him in newness of life; the law of
God is written on my heart, not on tables of stone.'

   'Nevertheless I live, yet not I, but Christ liveth in me. I live
spiritually; and it is not the same "I" as before, but a new man,
a new creature' (2 Cor. 5:17). This new man lives by faith,
looking to Christ for all things — pardon, righteousness, peace,
joy, comfort and the supply of every grace.

v.21.   'I do not despise, reject, nor make void the grace of
God in Christ Jesus. If a justifying righteousness comes through
obedience to the ceremonial law, then Christ died in vain.' If
obedience to the law is necessary for a man to be justified
before God, then all that Christ did was in vain; for no man
will be justified!

The just shall live by faith

Galatians 3:1-12

v.1.   'Foolish Galatians.' Any man is foolish who leaves Christ
to go to Moses, who leaves the gospel of grace to go to the
working of the law, who leaves the doctrine of free justification
(which gives peace and comfort) to go to the law (which can
only condemn and bring bondage).

'Who hath deceived you? The truth of Christ crucified has been set forth in your hearing. Who Christ is, what Christ has done, why Christ suffered and where Christ is now was faithfully preached to you.' It wasn't as if they had not heard the gospel. They had heard, claimed to believe and now were going back to the works of the law (2 Cor. 11:3).

v.2.   He could ask them many things, but he asked this one question only, which, if rightly attended to and honestly answered, must expose their foolishness and put an end to the controversy: '**Did you receive the Spirit of God by the works of the law or by the hearing of faith?** Did the Spirit of God (as the Spirit of regeneration, of wisdom, of understanding, of adoption and the earnest of future glory) come to you through your obedience to the law, or did he come to you when you heard the good news of Christ in the gospel and received that gospel by faith?' There is only one answer (Eph. 2:8,9; Rom. 10:17).

v.3.   'Is it possible that you can be so foolish as to think:
    1. That having been chosen in Christ by grace you are kept in Christ by works?
    2. That having begun your Christian life depending on the Spirit and the grace of God you must finish it depending on your own works and flesh?
    3. That having been accepted in the Beloved, you are not made perfect until you add your own righteousness to his?' This is unthinkable! (Heb. 12:2; Phil. 1:6.)

v.4.   These Galatians had suffered great reproach for the gospel of grace (persecutions and afflictions), as all who embrace it expect to do! Now if this gospel of pure grace in Christ is not true, then you have suffered all these afflictions needlessly. He adds, 'I hope that you will correct your mistake and abide by the gospel, that your suffering be not in vain.'

v.5.   These Galatians had not only received the Spirit of God through hearing and believing the gospel, but they had seen the gospel confirmed by extraordinary gifts, signs and wonders

of the Holy Spirit, who was also still among them (Heb. 2:3,4).
Now the apostle asks, 'Did he who gave you the Spirit and he
who worked these miracles do so attending the preaching of
the law or the preaching of the gospel?' (Mark 16:15-18.)

v.6.   Abraham was a righteous man, head of the Jewish
nation, the first of the circumcision and one in whom the false
Jewish teachers gloried (and would persuade the Gentiles to
the practice of circumcision in imitation of Abraham); but the
apostle shows that Abraham was justified before God by faith,
not by circumcision (Rom. 4:9-11, 21-23).

v.7.   Those who are of the same faith as Abraham (not of the
same degree, but exercised on the same object — Jehovah the
Word, the Lord our Righteousness, and wrought by the same
Spirit), they are the true children of Abraham, for he is the
father of all that believe, whether Jew or Gentile.

vv.8,9.   The Word of God is represented as declaring the
purpose of God before it comes to pass, and the Word of God
declared to Abraham that in his seed should all nations be
blessed. This seed is Christ! (Gal. 3:16; Rom. 4:13,16.) The
gospel of righteousness in and through Christ was preached to
Abraham that the Messiah would spring through him, and in
the Messiah all nations would be blessed (Gen. 12:3).

v.10.   As many as seek for justification by the works and
deeds of the law and trust their own works and righteousness
for acceptance with God are under the curse of the law; for
the law requires doing — not knowing, or hearing, or approving,
but perfectly doing all that the law requires in word, thought
and deed (Gal. 4:21; Rom. 10:1-4).

v.11.   There were many justified before the law was given,
such as Abel, Noah, Enoch, Job, Abraham and all other
believers; and there were many justified during the legal
dispensation; but none was justified by his obedience to the
law. The law was not given to save, but to reveal sin, to lead us
to Christ (the types were given to reveal Christ). Furthermore,

no man ever perfectly kept the law. The Scriptures declare, 'The just shall live by faith' (Hab. 2:4; Rom. 1:17; Heb. 10:38).

v.12. The law is not of faith, nor does it require faith, but it requires perfect obedience by the man. The law reaches not only to the outward man but to the inward parts, requiring not only external obedience but perfect thought, motive and attitude!

Justification by promise - not by law

Galatians 3:13-29

v.13. In the preceding verses Paul shows the law to be a cursing law because of its perfection and the imperfection of our nature and deeds. Therefore, no man can be justified by a law of works. In this verse he shows us how we are justified and redeemed from the curse of the law. Christ was made a curse for us (Gal. 4:4,5; Isa. 53:4-6). Cursed is everyone who is hanged for crime (Deut. 21:22,23).

v.14. 'That the blessing of Abraham' — the same blessing of justification (imputed righteousness before God) which Abraham had in Christ — 'might come on the Gentiles' (Rom. 4:7-10). Abraham was not justified by law, works, nor circumcision but by Christ (Rom. 4:20-25). We receive the realization of the promise of the Spirit by faith. The Holy Spirit opens and applies the promises of God. Justification, then, is not by law but is by faith in Christ because it was purchased by Christ.

In verses 15-18 the apostle argues that justification before God cannot be by the law because these promises were made by God in a covenant 430 years before the Levitical law was given.

1. Justification is not by law because the law says, 'Do and live.' Man cannot fulfil the holy law, so the law only condemns.

2. Justification is not by law but in Christ, who redeemed us from the curse of the law by the sacrifice of himself.

3. Justification is not by law since it was promised by God in a covenant of mercy before the law was given.

v.15.   A covenant or testament made by a man cannot be overturned or disannulled when it is confirmed; much less can the covenant of God be disannulled or cancelled.

v.16.   These promises of acceptance, justification and eternal life were made not to Christ personally, not to all the natural seed of Abraham, but to Christ's body, the church, the spiritual seed of Abraham, both Jews and Gentiles. The promises are made to all believers, who are one in Christ!

v.17.   The Levitical law, which was given 430 years after the covenant concerning the Messiah (Gen. 12:1-3), does not and cannot change or make void the promise of life in Christ by faith.

v.18.   If justification is by keeping the law or by ceremony, it cannot be of promise; but God gave it to Abraham by promise.

v.19.   What was the purpose of the law?
1. It was given after the promise in order to reveal and expose to men their guilt and to make men more conscious of the sinfulness of sin.
2. It was given to reveal the Messiah, the Redeemer, in types and pictures until he came (Heb. 10:1).
3. Moses served as the mediator between Israel and God (Exod. 20:18,19). He was a type (a picture) of Christ, our Mediator. The angels of God were messengers and instruments God used in the giving of the law.

v.20.   A mediator has to do with more than one party. There can be no mediator if only one person is involved. Yet God is only one person; he is the one offended, standing off at a distance, giving the law in the hands of a mediator, revealing their alienation. Therefore, justification cannot be expected through the law.

v.21.   Is the law against or opposed to the promises of God?
Of course not! The giving of the moral law and the ceremonial
law does not change the promise of life in Christ. If a law
could be given that would justify a sinner, then justification
would be by that law.

v.22.   But the Word of God, especially the law of God,
pictures all mankind as sinners shut up and imprisoned by sin
so that the blessing of life must come through Christ, the
Messiah, to them that believe (Rom. 8:1-3).

vv.23,24.   But until Christ, the object of faith, came to fulfil
the law, we were kept under the law which served as a tutor or
an instructor to show us our sins, to reveal God's mercy in
Christ and to instruct us in the justice and righteousness of
God. The law empties the sinner of all self, glory and merit
and brings him to Christ, the Justifier.

vv.25,26.   After Christ came, we are no longer under these
types, pictures and ceremonies; but in Christ we are sons of
God, justified, forgiven and righteous. The law has served its
purpose and is put away (Heb. 10:8-10).

vv.27-29.   'As many of you (Jew or Gentile, male or female,
slave or free) who have been baptized by the Spirit of God
into a spiritual union with Jesus Christ are one in Christ. All
that Christ is, you are. All that Christ has, you have. You are
accepted in the Beloved!'

Christ redeemed us from the law

Galatians 4:1-11

In these verses Paul deals with the annulment of the ceremonial law under which the Old Testament people were as children under a tutor; he blames the Gentile believers for returning to that law when they had been freed from it!

vv.1,2. To illustrate what he said in Galatians 3:23,24, Paul presents the case of an heir during his childhood. The heir is owner and lord of all by promise and testament; yet while he is a child and under age, he is not his own man. He is under restraint, kept in school, taught and corrected as if he were a servant and not the heir. The father appoints a time for his inheritance to come into effect.

v.3. Even so the Jews, when they were children in spiritual knowledge (in the infant state of the church), were kept like children in school under the ceremonies, sacrifices and rituals of the Mosaic law. These are called 'elements of the world' because they lay in outward, worldly and earthly things such as animal sacrifices, washings, meats, etc.

vv.4,5. But when the time appointed by the Father was fulfilled, he sent his Son, the Lord Jesus Christ, the Messiah, into the world.
   1. **Made of a woman** — not created as Adam or begotten of man as all other men are, but conceived by the Holy Spirit in a virgin's womb. He was made flesh and he identified with us in every respect.
   2. **Made under the law** — under the civil and judicial law as a Jew, under the ceremonial law as a son of Abraham and under the moral law as a man and the Surety of his people.
   3. **To redeem them** — by meeting and obeying the law in

every jot and tittle. By going to the cross and suffering the penalty of our sins, Christ purchased our freedom, redeemed us from the curse of the law and satisfied the justice of God that we might receive the power and privilege of sons of God (John 1:12,13; Gal. 3:13).

v.6. 'Now because you are truly sons of God (accepted in the Beloved, redeemed from all sin, having no condemnation), God has put his Spirit of adoption, of assurance, of comfort, of holiness in your heart whereby you can actually call God your loving Father.'

The word 'Abba' is a Hebrew word meaning father. It may be that the word is in both Hebrew and Greek to show that God is the Father of both Jew and Gentile believers.

v.7. Therefore, we are no longer servants under tutors, schoolmasters, ceremonies and types; but we are sons of God who have been made free from the law and have entered into the joy and enjoyment of all blessings of redemption in Christ (1 Cor. 1:30; Col. 2:8-11).

v.8. 'When you Gentiles knew not the true God, you worshipped idols and were in bondage to gods that did not exist; they were of this world and the product of your imagination. You performed rites and ceremonies that were useless.'

v.9. 'Now after God has revealed himself to you in Christ Jesus and you know the true and living God (who chose you and foreknew you), why do you turn back to rituals, ceremonies and elementary, worthless things, such as circumcision, holy days and foods and drinks which can do nothing for you before God?' Paul is astonished that these professed believers would want to be in bondage to things from which Christ had set them free.

v.10. By 'days' he means seventh-day sabbaths. The sabbath was typical of Christ, who is the true rest of his people.

'Months', designs new moons, or the beginning of months. These were kept by holding religious feasts and abstaining from work.

'Times' mean the three times during the year that the
Jewish males appeared before the Lord at Jerusalem to keep
the three feasts — Tabernacle, Passover and Pentecost.

'Years' are to indicate sabbatical years. Every seventh year
the fields were to be idle — no ploughing or planting. Paul
blamed these Gentiles because they were being drawn into
these practices to obtain acceptance with God (Gal. 5:1,2).

v.11.   Paul knew that the true minister of God never labours
in vain (Isa. 49:5; 2 Cor. 2:14-16). He speaks with reference to
them. If they should persist in bringing in the ceremonies,
circumcision and observance of these laws to make effectual
the redemptive work of Christ, then for them the gospel is
preached in vain. Salvation cannot be by grace and by works
(Gal. 2:21; 5:1-4).

Christ formed in you

Galatians 4:12-20

v.12.   'Become as Paul, free from the bondage of ritualism
and ceremonies. Reckon yourselves to be dead to the Levitical
laws which have been fulfilled by Christ. Count these things as
loss and rubbish for Christ.'

'I have become as you are (Gentiles) with respect to things
spiritual. We are both alike in Christ — chosen in him, redeemed
in him, perfected in him and free from the observance of
ceremonies and laws. You have not injured me by your law
observances. The offence is against Christ, who fulfilled the
law. My feelings for you have not changed, but your feelings
toward me have' (Gal. 1:6).

vv.13-16.   'When I first preached the gospel of God's grace to
you, I did so in much weakness, humility, persecution and
bodily afflictions. You were not offended by my bodily
ailments nor my sufferings' (what they were we do not know);

'but you were so glad to hear the good news of Christ that you received me as an angel of God, even as Christ himself. What has become of that respect and regard you had for me? You would have given me your very eyes' (this is what led many to believe that the apostle had severe eye trouble). What Paul is saying is that these people were happy in Christ (in the gospel of free grace); and now that the law-preachers had influenced them, they had not only turned from the gospel of Christ alone but had become Paul's enemies. 'Am I your enemy because I tell you the truth and deal sincerely with you? Am I your enemy because I preach that we are complete in Christ and have no need to be circumcised, to keep days, months and years?'

v.17. 'These false preachers are courting you, pretending great love and concern for you, making much of you; but their purpose is not for God's glory nor your eternal good. What they are trying to do is to exclude me or to isolate you from me and other true apostles, that you might follow them and bring them great favour and success' (2 Peter 2:1-3). The zeal and enthusiasm of the false preachers was not to turn the Galatians to Christ but to win popular applause unto themselves.

v.18. Paul does not condemn all zeal and affection, but only that which has an ulterior motive and objective. It is good to be zealous and extremely dedicated if our zeal is toward Christ and the gospel. The godly zeal and affection for the gospel and one another was to be constant, continuous and not only when he was present with them. He loved them and desired their salvation, sanctification and peace in Christ, not only when he was there but when he was away. It seemed that when he was there, they were attached to him and the truth; but when he left, their affection cooled and they turned to others.

> Content with beholding his face, my all to his pleasure resigned,
> No changes of season or place would make any change in my mind.

v.19. 'My little children.' Paul speaks to the Galatians most affectionately as a father to his sons. They were sons of God and were still babes in Christ; consequently, the term 'little children' was appropriate; but they were also 'Paul's children', for he was the instrument God used to bring them to faith in Christ.

'Of whom I travail in birth again.' He compares himself to a woman with child. All of his pains, sufferings and labours in the ministry of the gospel he compares to the sorrows of a woman during the time of child-bearing. The woman is concerned, dedicated and involved in one purpose; and that is to bring forth a living child. She counts her suffering and pains worthwhile if she can produce a living, healthy child. The apostle had not thought for himself but for them. All that he was concerned about and dedicated to in prayer, preaching and suffering was that Christ might be formed in them.

'Until Christ be formed in you.' This is the same as to be saved, to be a new creature in Christ Jesus!

1. A form of religion, with its laws, ordinances and ceremonies, is not eternal life.

2. A form of morality, with its fleshly 'do's and 'do not's is not eternal life.

3. A form of profession, with its decisions, baptisms and creeds is not eternal life. 'Eternal life is to know God and Jesus Christ, whom he hath sent,' to have the *life* of Christ, the *presence* of Christ, the *Spirit and mind* of Christ and the *very glory* of Christ begotten, created and formed in us (Gal. 2:20). Until this is done and unless this miracle of grace is accomplished, our religion is vain. It is no more than that of the Pharisees of old, of whom Christ said, 'They neither know me nor my Father.' Salvation is Christ in you; the hope of glory is Christ in you; the life of God is Christ in you (1 John 5:11,12).

v.20. 'I wish I could be present with you in person that I might exhort you face to face. Your concern about circumcision, holy days and ceremonies makes me fearful of your knowledge of Christ and causes me to doubt your real interest in Christ.' A union with Christ produces fruit and evidences; and when these fruits and evidences are absent, true ministers of the gospel are concerned for the spiritual well-being of their hearers. When the lordship and sufficiency of Christ wane in a person, there is ample reason to question his profession.

Born free

Galatians 4:21-31

These verses present an allegory or a story in which people, things and happenings have a symbolic meaning. Abraham had two sons — one by a servant maid, the other by his wife. Hagar, the servant, represented the covenant at Mount Sinai; Sarah, the free woman, represented the covenant of grace and the gospel church state. Also, their two sons represented two sorts of professors — legalists and evangelical Christians. True believers in Christ are like Isaac, children of promise; legalists are like Ishmael, men after the flesh.

v.21. 'Tell me, you that seek to be justified by the law and seek acceptance with God by obedience to the law, do you not hear what the law really says? The law never speaks peace or pardon but declares us all to be guilty (Rom. 3:19,20). It sentences us to wrath and condemnation. Do you want to be under such a law?'

vv.22,23. Abraham had two sons. Ishmael was born of a servant, so he was but a servant himself and not the heir. Isaac was born of a free woman who was joined in the family with her husband; therefore, Isaac was no servant but a free man, even the heir. A second principle is here intended. Ishmael was **'born after the flesh'**, or by the ordinary strength of nature (his mother being a young woman fit for conception). Isaac was not conceived from such a principle. His mother was ninety years old and unable to bear children, so he was born 'by promise', or by the miracle of God.

vv.24,25.   These two women represent the two covenants.

1. The covenant of grace under the old administration, which was greatly mistaken (it was never given to save) and was degenerated into a covenant of works by those who adhered to it.

2. The covenant of grace under the new administration (Heb. 8:7,8).

The Sinai covenant was prefigured by Hagar, the servant, by the effect which it produces if life and acceptance are sought by it. It produces children of bondage! It cannot produce heirs of life. It speaks of human works, merit and fear and is, like Jerusalem today, in bondage to the law, sin and the wrath of God. Followers of the law can no more be heirs of God than Ishmael, son of the bondswoman, can be the true heir of Abraham. He will always be the servant, not the son.

v.26.   Here Paul describes the covenant of grace in Christ — our Mediator, our Representative, our sin-offering. The messianic kingdom of Christ is from above, not from Sinai. The righteousness is in his obedience, not in ours. Its redemption is in his sacrifice and his satisfaction, not in the ordinances of the tabernacle. Its access to the throne of God is through Christ, our great High Priest, not through an earthly priesthood! This covenant is free from the curse of the law and from the bondage of the law and is the mother of every believer, Jew and Gentile. We are born of grace.

v.27.   This is a prophecy from Isaiah 54:1 and seems to refer to the church as it was in the early days after our Lord's death and under the ministry of the apostles. There were a few believers in a few cities, but the Lord promises that she shall be a fruitful mother with many children.

v.28.   We believers are the children of promise, as Isaac was.

1. As Isaac was promised to Abraham, we were promised and given to the Lord Jesus Christ (John 6:37-39; Eph. 1:3,4).

2. As Isaac was conceived and born beyond the strength

and course of nature, we are born spiritually by the power of God (John 1:12,13).

3. As Isaac was the heir by birth as the son of Abraham, we are heirs of God and joint-heirs with Christ (Rom. 8:16,17).

v.29. Ishmael, the son of flesh, mocked and persecuted the son of promise. Even so, the false prophets of justification by works and advocates of the Levitical law for acceptance with God will and do mock and persecute all who trust and rest only in Christ for justification and redemption. Salvation by works and salvation by grace are opposite and contrary. True believers mock and persecute no one, but those who trust in their works and deeds have always hated and persecuted children of promise.

v.30. Ishmael, the child of flesh and works, had to be cast out along with the mother who produced him. He could not be an heir with the true son. Even so, the system of works and human merit must be forsaken from our hearts, from our churches and from our fellowship, along with the children of flesh which this system produces. The heirs of God are the children of his grace in Christ Jesus. The self-righteous, the justified by works, the part-Christ-and-part-flesh advocates *cannot* be heirs with children of promise.

v.31. 'So then, we who are born again are not children of the law, of the natural flesh; but we are supernatural children of free grace. To God be all the glory!'

The liberty of grace

Galatians 5:1-12

v.1. We are told by the apostle to 'stand fast in' (highly esteem, maintain, defend) the liberty of Christ, of grace, of the gospel. Christ has freed us from:

1. *Sin* — not from the indwelling of it nor the temptation to it, but from the guilt of it, the dominion of it and the damning power of it.

2. *The ceremonial law* — from circumcision, sacrifices, feast days, sabbath days and all of its burdensome rites and ceremonies.

3. *The moral law* as a covenant of works — from its curse and condemnation, but not from obedience to it as held forth by our Lord Jesus.

Christ has given us a free use of the gospel ordinances, free access to the throne of grace and a freedom from fear of death and judgement. 'Don't allow anyone to entangle you again with a system of works and deeds in order to obtain God's favour.' We are complete in Christ.

v.2.   If a man submits to circumcision in order to gain acceptance with God, Christ profits him nothing. Christ must be received as our only and sufficient Redeemer. If we add anything (even if performed in a religious way) to the person and work of Christ to gain God's favour, whether it be circumcision, baptism, feasting, praying at certain times, or doing good for others, we are not fully trusting and resting in Christ. Therefore, he profits us nothing, for we are attempting to add our righteousness to his. This is to show contempt for him.

v.3.   If we are going to seek any measure of righteousness by works and obedience to laws, we are not depending fully on Christ and are, therefore, under obligation to obey perfectly the complete law, both ceremonial and moral.

v.4.   Keep this verse in its context! Remember to whom it is spoken and for what reason. 'You, who seek to be justified before God by your own righteousness and obedience to certain laws, such as circumcision, sabbath days, washings and abstaining from certain food, have turned away from the gospel of free grace and righteousness in Christ. You have departed from salvation by grace alone and have turned to a mixture of grace and works; therefore, Christ is become of no effect to you at all!' Christ is our whole Saviour or not our

Saviour at all. He will not share his glory (Rom. 4 :3-5; 11:5,6).

v.5. By the Holy Spirit's regeneration, revelation and help (not relying on our works, deeds, nor obedience to the law), we anticipate and wait for the fulfilment of that blessed hope of eternal glory which our right standing before God and our righteousness in Christ promise us. Our hope is in Christ, not in any deeds or works of the law.

v.6. If we are in Christ by grace and faith, it does not profit us one thing to be circumcised or uncircumcised! To observe or not to observe these things commanded in the Levitical law does not commend us to God. The service which God requires is a true heart of faith, which is evidenced and expressed by our love to Christ and to one another.

vv. 7, 8. 'You started well in the beginning. You came as helpless sinners to Christ; you found in him all you need; you were zealous for the gospel of grace. Who turned you back to the law? Who hindered you in your faith? Who turned you to another gospel? It was not God (who called you by grace) nor Christ (who fulfilled all things for you) nor the Holy Spirit (who revealed the gospel) nor an apostle of Christ (who preached the gospel to you). It was Satan and his messengers of human righteousness' (2 Cor. 11:2,3, 13-15).

v.9. Someone may say, 'There's no need for Paul to become so upset. We do not embrace the whole Jewish economy, only circumcision and a ceremony here and a sabbath day there.' Paul reminds them that a little leaven (error, evil, especially in regard to the work of Christ) will pervert and mislead the whole church. It must be stamped out immediately!

v.10. The apostle has dealt roughly and plainly with them, yet he expresses confidence in them that they will see what he is teaching and deal with these false teachers. They shall hear their judgement from the church and from the Lord.

v.11. Some of these false teachers contended that Paul

taught that circumcision was necessary to salvation, since he had had Timothy circumcised (Acts 16:3). We know why Paul did this — to prevent the stumbling of weak Jews and to enable Timothy (a Gentile) to preach to them. It was *not* for his spiritual good.

1. 'If I am an advocate of circumcision and other laws, why do these men persecute and constantly oppose me?'

2. 'If I preach circumcision or any other work added to the person and work of Christ, the doctrine of the cross as an offence and as a stumbling-block would cease.' Men do not object to Christ's being a part Saviour. It is Christ the total and complete Saviour that they deny.

v.12.   Paul is speaking here of the false teachers (Gal. 1:8,9).

Walk in the Spirit - not in the flesh

Galatians 5:13-26

v.13.   In Christ (by the Spirit of God) every believer has been called (not only externally but internally) out of bondage to sin, Satan and the law and into the liberty of Christ and the gospel. Christ has made us free from days, ceremonies, sacrifices, circumcision and external rituals. We are complete in him. Yet the doctrine of Christian liberty may be abused, if we use it as an excuse to fulfil the lusts of the flesh, if we forget the rules of moderation, or if we make our liberty a stumbling-block to weak Christians. We are to be directed in all that we do by a love for Christ and a love for others, especially for those who are babes in Christ (Rom. 14:13-16; 1 Cor. 8:9-13; 10:23, 28-33).

v.14.   The moral laws of God are separated into two parts: my duties toward God and my duties toward men. These laws are fulfilled in this: 'love to God and love to men' (Matt. 22:37-40). When I consider what I can do, should do and am required to do in word, thought and deed toward others, it is all fulfilled in the word 'love' (Matt. 7:12). My love for the Lord will control my personal conduct and behaviour, and my love for others will control my public conduct where others are concerned. As far as a man loves aright, so far he fulfils the law.

v.15. 'If you are critical, unforgiving, unkind and filled with bitterness and division, you will destroy the unity, peace and followship of the church; for love is the cement that binds us together' (Col. 3:12-14).

v.16. **'Walk in the Spirit.'**
   1. In the Holy Spirit of truth; for he guides us in all truth, revealing the Word he has written.
   2. In the Spirit of Christ as our example (Phil. 2:5-7).
   3. In the spirit of love, exercising the fruit of the Holy Spirit (Gal. 5:22). And though the lust of the flesh is ever present, we shall not give way to it, nor be overcome by it. The presence of the flesh does not mean that it must be served.

v.17. **'The flesh'** is the corruption of nature which is still in every believer. **'The spirit'** is the internal principle of grace and divine life that is born in us by the Spirit of God. These are contrary, or as opposite as light and darkness. They are enemies! One seeks to hurt or destroy the other, **'so that you cannot do the things that you would,'** which is understood of both evil and good! The believer would do perfectly good (this is his desire), yet he cannot because of a nature of sin which still abides. His old nature would do all evil, but it cannot because of the divine nature that is ever present! (Rom. 7:15-17, 22,23.)

v.18. We are led by the Spirit of God to the Word of God:
   1. to the Lord Jesus Christ;
   2. to the throne of grace;
   3. to the duties of love and grace;
   4. to a new life of fellowship with God.
   It is not the law which is our leader and our inspiration, but the Holy Spirit. Men are not motivated to love and righteousness by law, but by the Holy Spirit.

vv.19-21.   'In the flesh dwelleth no good thing.' Understand
that these sinful practices are characteristic of the flesh, and
though we have done these things and the potential to do
them is still present in our flesh (as evidenced by Abraham,
David, Lot, Peter), yet this is not our pattern of life, not the
practice of the believer! Our tenor of life and the bent of our
wills is holiness, righteousness and peace. Those who would
still live by these principles and practices of the flesh are not
redeemed and shall not inherit the kingdom of God.

vv.22,23.   Notice the word is **'fruit,'** not 'fruits'. This fruit is
not of nature, nor flesh, but is the result of the indwelling
Spirit and that which is produced by him. We can take no
glory for any good or good works that are in us, for these are
all by his grace. But this fruit, in various degrees according to
our spiritual growth, is in every believer.

v.24.   The people who belong to Christ (who have been
redeemed by his blood and indwelt by his Spirit) have put and
are putting to death these works of the flesh. They have
declared war on their natural flesh and the sins of the flesh and
will have Christ, not sin, to reign over them.

v.25.   If we live by the Spirit of grace, if we have been made
alive to God by his power and presence, let us also walk daily
by his help, assistance, influence and direction. We begin in the
Spirit and we are sanctified daily by the Spirit of God.

v.26.   We are not desirous of honour, esteem and applause
from men, for 'we are what we are by the grace of God'. God
can take away what we have as easily as he gave it. We do not
despise and provoke one another with our piety; nor do we
want to appear to be wiser, richer in grace, nor more gifted
than others, for we are less than the least of the saints. Nor do
we envy the gifts, abilities, or grace of another. God will
enlighten us, equip us and bless us as he sees fit to use us.

Some good advice

Galatians 6:1-10

In this section the apostle deals with several areas that are most important to those who know and love the Saviour.

1. Our attitude toward those who stumble and fall.
2. Our love for one another and our identification with those in trial.
3. Our humility and genuine modesty.
4. Our generosity and willingness to share what we have.

v.1. We are redeemed, children of God, indwelt by his Spirit of holiness and grace; but we are still human, still flesh. The motions of sin, the desires of the flesh and the potential to fall are in every believer. Therefore, if a brother falls into sin of spirit, attitude, or flesh, we are to make every attempt to recover, restore and resettle him to his place of fellowship. The attitude of strong, mature, restrained believers toward the fallen is not to be critical, 'holier than thou' and condemning. It is to be a spirit of humility and meekness, for we know that the potential to commit any sin is in us, and we only stand by the grace of God! (2 Tim. 2:24,25.)

v.2. 'Bear one another's frailties, infirmities and weaknesses' (and we all have them). 'Don't desert, withdraw fellowship and condemn.' 'Love beareth all things.' Bear these burdens by comforting the brother while gently reproving him. Sympathize with and forgive him in genuine mercy. In doing so we will fulfil the royal law of Christ (John 13:34).

v.3. 'Man at his best state is altogether vanity.' 'In my flesh dwelleth no good thing.' I owe my being, my knowledge, my mercies, my preservation and my gifts to God alone (1 Cor. 4:7). In myself and left to myself I am nothing and know nothing. Now if in pride and self-esteem I think myself to be something, I am deceived. Pride of face, race, place, or grace is an abomination to God (Prov. 6:16-18).

vv.4,5. These two verses must be considered in the context! It is so easy to compare ourselves with weaker Christians, less gifted believers, or even fallen brothers, and to begin to think that we are something special, we are strong, or we are better than others. We are not to prove ourselves by other men's sins or actions, but in the light of God's glory and holiness. If we can find some measure of genuine spiritual growth and some evidence of the fruit of the Spirit, we can rejoice in what God has truly been pleased to do for and in us, rather than being buoyed up in vain hope simply because we are not as other men. Every man is judged according to his own works, not in a comparative view of others.

v.6. This verse has to do with the support of those who preach and teach the Word of God. They that preach the gospel as pastors, evangelists and missionaries are to be supported and cared for by those whom they teach. The doctor who ministers to you, the policeman who protects you, the carpenter who builds for you are all compensated according to their service. Even so, the man who studies, prays for and teaches you the Word of God (the most important service) is to share in your material substance.

v.7. Do not be deceived by a covetous heart or by false teachers! Our God is not to be mocked; and withholding those things which are needed from his true ministers because of covetousness, ingratitude, or indifference is to mock God. He has, from the early days, ordained that those who minister in things of the temple shall partake of those things. 'What a man sows he reaps.' This is a proverbial expression that applies to all actions, good and bad. If a man sows wheat, he reaps wheat. If a man sows nothing, he reaps nothing (2 Cor. 9:5-8).

v.8. If a man is only concerned for his physical and material welfare, if he devotes all his possessions to pamper, please and provide for his body, he will reap the dividends of the flesh — corruption! It will all decay, rot and be food for worms. But if a man uses his time, strength and substance for the glory of God and for the good of his soul and the souls of others, he will reap everlasting happiness (Matt. 6:19-21).

v.9. If what we do and give is according to the will of God, out of a principle of love to him, for the glory of God and in the name of the Lord Jesus, we need not grow weary nor discouraged. In God's own time, either in this world or in the world to come, we shall see the fruit of our labours of love. Let us not be impatient but wait on the Lord.

v.10. As we have the opportunity and the ability, and as the occasion requires, let us do good to all men (strangers, neighbours, believers and unbelievers), but especially let us care for, encourage and assist those who are believers with us in Christ Jesus.

And in conclusion . . .

Galatians 6:11-18

v.11. The apostle had great affection for the believers at Galatia. The errors to which they had been exposed, and into which many had fallen, caused him great grief, so he says, 'Take notice of the *length* of this epistle and the fact that it is written *in my own hand*.' There were longer epistles, but most of them had been dictated by Paul and written by someone else (Rom. 16:22). Oh, for a heart that cares for others and that is broken when their peace is threatened by error or sin!

v.12. Paul's chief purpose in this epistle was to expose the false teachers and their errors, so he cannot conclude without taking some further notice of them, which he does by exposing their hypocrisy and ambition.

1. They do what they do to be seen of men. Their religion is an outward show (Matt. 6:1-5) and only exists in the observance of days, circumcision and laws respecting foods and drinks. They congratulate one another on their spirituality and devotion to religious practices.

2. 'They want you to adopt their ceremonies and legalistic rules lest they suffer persecution from the religious Jews,' who were offended at the preaching of the total sufficiency of Christ. Christ crucified is our atonement, and Christ's obedience is our righteousness, without any part of the Levitical law to be added. To be saved a man has only to look by faith to Christ, not to be baptized, circumcised, observe a day, join a church, or keep a law. 'We are complete in him!'

v. 13.   'These religious teachers, who preach the law, teach the law and boast of their regard for the law, do not keep the whole law.' This the flesh cannot do, and to bring in one part of the law for righteousness or justification before God requires us to keep the whole law perfectly. 'But they require you Gentiles to submit to circumcision, so that they can boast before the other Jews of the number of proselytes or converts they have won to their brand of religion or system of salvation. Every religious person glories or rejoices in something. These false teachers glory in the flesh, in the outward form, in the noise they make, in the work they do and in the souls they have won.

v. 14.   Paul says, **'I glory in the cross of Christ.'** My chief glory, rejoicing and delight are in the person and work of Christ, not in myself, my works, nor even in whatever God is pleased to do through me, but in Christ alone!' He gloried not in the wood of the cross but in the person who suffered on that tree and the effects of his obedience and sacrifice. Christ is our wisdom, righteousness, sanctification and redemption.

'The world is crucified unto me. I do not fear men nor what they can do any more than I would fear one nailed to a tree. The ceremonial law is nailed to his cross. The world, its riches, honours, applause, pleasures and profits are also nailed to that cross. I am no more drawn to them than I would be to a convicted felon nailed to a cross.'

'**I am crucified to the world**.' The world had no affection
for him, and he had none for the world. 'You can count me
out of your plans; I am dead to your whole philosophy and
system.' The ceremonial law was dead to Paul, and Paul was
dead to it. He would have nothing to do with these beggarly
elements.

v.15.   Circumcision and obedience to any of the rituals and
ceremonies can profit you nothing before God for justification
and righteousness. Abstinence from these rituals and ceremonies can profit you nothing. That which is profitable and of
eternal value is '**a new creature**'. The new creature consists of a
new spiritual man in Christ Jesus, a new glory of Christ motivated by a real love for him.

v.16.   This is the rule of our walk and conduct: to renounce
all trust in and dependence upon any outward thing, to believe
alone in Christ for righteousness, to walk in love, holiness and
newness of life under the influence of his Spirit and grace!
(2 Cor. 5:14,15.)

v.17.   The false apostles boast of their circumcision made by
their own hands; but Paul holds up the real scars in his body,
made by stonings, beatings, imprisonment and the sufferings
which he endured for preaching the gospel of Christ. Like a
soldier who holds up the stub of an arm lost in battle to show
his devotion and bravery, Paul says, 'Don't bother me any
more with your false claims of will-worship and righteousness
by the law.' Preach Christ crucified and sufferings will follow.

v.18.   Paul closes with his usual benediction, expressing his
love for them as brethren and wishing for them the best
blessing of God, the grace of Christ, that this might be in their
hearts and spirits!

Ephesians

God's free grace in Christ

Ephesians 1:1-14

In order to help us in our study of the first part of chapter 1, I will divide it into five parts.

I   *vv.1, 2.*   The salutation or greeting. The writer is **'Paul'**. His office is **'an apostle of Jesus Christ'**. His call to that office is **'by the will of God'**. The people to whom he writes are **'the saints at Ephesus, the faithful in Christ Jesus'**. His prayer for them is for **'grace and peace from the Father and the Lord Jesus'**.

II   *v.3.*   The ground and cause of the salvation of sinners is the free grace of God in Christ. God is the God of Christ, as Christ is man and Mediator, and God is the Father of Christ, as Christ is God by an eternal and unspeakable generation (Ps. 2:7). **'Blessed be God**, that is, we congratulate his greatness and goodness; we ascribe glory and honour to him and give thanks for all **'spiritual blessings'**. These spiritual blessings are more than common or temporal blessings. They are 'special' blessings. They are mercy and grace through the eternal covenant, all things pertaining to justification, peace, pardon, adoption, sanctification and eternal life! **'In Christ'** God has purposed, decreed and given every spiritual blessing which heaven can bestow, which heaven can require and which is needed to enter and enjoy heaven's realm. Praise God for all that I am, have and ever shall be! It is his gift through my Head and Representative, the Lord Jesus Christ.

III   *vv.4-6.*   Paul deals with the means of salvation as they were purposed, decreed and prepared by the Father in his eternal counsel.
   1. The Father *chose* us in Christ before the foundation of

the world, not because we were holy, but that we should be
holy. God, in eternity past, determined to have a holy people
to populate a new heaven and a new earth; therefore, he chose
them in Christ out of Adam's fallen race (John 15:16; 2 Thess.
2:13; 2 Tim. 1:9; 1 Cor. 1:26-29).

2. The Father *predestinated* us to be adopted as his own
children through Jesus Christ (Acts 13:48; Rom. 8:29,30).
God foreordained the persons, the means and the end, or goal,
of redemption according to the good pleasure of his own will.

3. The Father *accepted* us in Christ, which is understood of
our persons as righteous, redeemed and sanctified in Christ. He
looks upon us in Christ and is well pleased. We are already
seated with Christ in heavenly places (Eph. 2:6). All of this
God the Father has done for the eternal praise of his glorious
grace (Eph. 2:7).

IV   *vv. 7-12.*   Paul deals with the means of salvation, as they
were purchased and accomplished by Christ in the work of
redemption.

1. Christ *redeemed* us by his blood. We were in bondage to
sin, the law and justice (Gal. 3:10). The law of God is honoured
by his obedience and the justice of God is satisfied by his
death, and we have full and complete forgiveness (Rom.
3:19-26).

2. Christ *enlightened* us as to the mystery of his gospel of
redemption. The gospel is a hidden mystery to the natural man,
Jew and Gentile (Col. 1:26; Rom. 16:25,26; 1 Cor. 2:7-10).
In Christ we see both the wisdom and the power of God in
redemption. This he reveals when he pleases and to whom he
pleases, that in his own time elect angels and elect men will be
brought together under one Head (Col. 1:16-18).

3. Christ *enriched* us. In Christ we were made God's children
and we obtained that glorious inheritance of all things (Rom.
8:16,17).

4. All of this Christ, our Redeemer, has done for the eternal
praise of his glorious grace (1 Cor. 1:30,31).

V   *vv. 13, 14.*   Paul deals in these verses with the means of
salvation as they are applied to the elect by the Holy Spirit.

1. We *heard* the gospel. This is hearing with the heart, the understanding and faith (Matt. 13:16,17; 1 Thess. 1:4,5). All men hear words, but the Holy Spirit quickens, regenerates and gives spiritual life to God's elect. They hear not just words, but truth — the good news of salvation.

2. We *believed* the gospel (Rom. 10:9,10, 13-15; Eph. 2:8,9). Faith is the gift and work of God in the soul.

3. We *were sealed* with the Holy Spirit. The seal or stamp of the eternal covenant is not circumcision, baptism, nor even our outward graces, but the Spirit of God (Rom. 8:9, 14-16; 1 John 3:24; 4:13).

4. The Holy Spirit is the guarantee of our inheritance. He is the first-fruits, the pledge and foretaste, the down payment on our inheritance. We have the indwelling Holy Spirit in anticipation of the full possession of our inheritance in God's good time. And all this he does to the praise of his glory.

Paul's prayer for the Ephesians

Ephesians 1:15-23

v.15.   Good reports had come to Paul of the Ephesians' 'faith in the Lord Jesus'. (They had seen the glory of his person and the fulness of his grace.) Paul also had heard of their love for all believers — Jew and Gentile, rich and poor, lesser and greater. Their faith was the cause of their love, the evidence of their justification (Rom. 5:1; John 13:35).

These two graces are inseparable. Faith and love go together and are found in the same persons. Where they exist, they cannot be hidden. Faith will confess and lean on Christ, and love will manifest itself in word and in deed (1 John 4:8).

v.16.   When we discover a work of God's grace in other people, it always leads us to two special responses:

1. We give thanks to God for them because this life and love in them is not a product of their merit but the gift of God.

2. We pray for them. We need to pray continually for one another as much after we are saved as before (1 Sam. 12:23).

In the next verses Paul gives us a summary of his prayers to God on their behalf.

1. *v.17.* **'That God may give you the Spirit of wisdom and revelation in the knowledge of him.'** These people already knew the Lord, as was indicated by their faith in him; but this is a prayer for the increase of that knowledge (2 Peter 3:18; Phil. 3:10). This knowledge of Christ and its increase can only come by and through the Holy Spirit, who is the Spirit of wisdom and revelation (John 16:13-15; 1 Cor. 2:10-13).

2. *v.18.* **'That the eyes of your understanding may be flooded with light and understanding'** — that you might see (1) the sinfulness of sin, (2) the insufficiency of your own righteousness, and (3) the beauty, glory and suitableness of Christ as Redeemer and Lord. The natural man, being in darkness, neither sees nor understands these mysteries (2 Cor. 4:3-6). We need a better view of them.

3. *v.18.* **'That you may know what is the hope of his calling.'** By which is meant either (1) the hope of external happiness, (2) Christ, who is our hope, (3) the grace of hope, which is an exercise of faith, or (4) all three! For the hope of eternal glory is founded on Christ, and the grace of hope lives only in the heart where Christ dwells! As we know more of Christ, we know more of the hope of his calling.

4. *v.18.* **'That ye may know the riches of the glory of his inheritance in the saints.'** The elect are the Lord's portion and inheritance, in whom he is glorified and will be glorified (Eph. 2:7). This seems to be speaking of the heavenly inheritance which the Lord is preparing for us (John 14:2,3). Paul said there are no words to describe it (2 Cor. 12:2-4).

5. *v.19.* **'That you may know the exceeding greatness of his power to us who believe.'** This is the power of God in our conversion and faith, the power that regenerated us, begat us,

raised us from the dead and formed Christ in us (Eph. 2:1; Col. 2:13).

v.20. This power of God that quickened us and made us to live spiritually is compared with that power which raised Christ from the dead. Christ was raised for our justification as our Representative. We live because he lives, and we are free from sin because our Surety, who bore our sins, is now free from them. But there is a likeness between his resurrection and our quickening.

1. His resurrection is called a begetting. He is the first-begotten from the dead. Our regeneration is termed a begetting (1 Peter 1:3).

2. His human body was lifeless, as natural men are without spiritual life.

3. His human body could not raise itself, as we cannot give ourselves life.

4. His resurrection was the pure, unaided work of God, as is our regeneration (Eph. 2:1).

5. His resurrection led to his exaltation at the right hand of God and is where in our representative (Christ) we who are regenerated are already seated! (Eph. 2:6.)

v.21. Christ, our Lord, is exalted far above all rule or authority, above all power and dominion in heaven, earth, or hell, and above every name that is named or title that can be conferred in this world or the world to come (Col. 1:16-18; Phil. 2:9-11). He has authority over all, especially his church!

vv.22,23. Christ has all authority (Matt. 28:18; John 17:2). Christ is the supreme Head of his church. This headship is an honourable, glorifying gift to him as Mediator. But it is also a grace gift to the church, for he rules for our good, he performs all offices for our salvation and he communicates all good things to us (Ps. 8:6).

Salvation by sovereign grace

Ephesians 2:1-10

In this portion of Scripture the apostle magnifies the riches of
God's grace in the salvation of sinners by Jesus Christ. He
describes what we were by nature (vv. 1-3). He then relates
what God has done for us in Christ (vv. 4,5). He next observes
our present and future blessings and glory (vv. 6-10).

v.1.   Every man by nature is dead in sin — separated from
God (v.12), without God, without Christ, without the Spirit,
completely deprived of any spiritual ability to do anything
good (Gen. 6:5; Jer. 13:23; Rom. 8:7; 3:10-12). The fountain
cause of this spiritual death was Adam's sin (Rom. 5:12, 17-19).
This corrupt state of sin and spiritual deadness is continued
through reproduction (Ps. 51:5; 58:3).

v.2.   Sins and evil are the path (road or direction) in which
all unbelievers walk. Walking denotes a continuous practice or
tenor of life. Sin was our daily employment and occupation.
In this walk of darkness we had two guides.
  1. '**According to the** corrupt **course** and custom **of the
world**.' The customs, manners and way of life of fallen flesh
determined our thoughts, values and conversation (Isa. 55:8;
1 Cor. 3:3). We walked as carnal men walk, not as spiritual
men walk.
  2. '**According to the prince of the power of the air**.' This is
Satan, who is called this, not because of any power he had
over winds, storms and weather, but because he is the prince
of a legion of demons and evil spirits who have residence in the
air. He has great power to blind men's minds, fill their hearts
with evil and lead them into great sin. Men walk after him,
imitate him and do his will (John 8:44). He reigns now in all
unbelievers.

v.3. The apostle says that in this condition, conduct and state we all (Jew and Gentile, himself included) lived and walked.

1. Our course of life was **'in the lusts of our flesh'**. This has to do mainly with the body — its appetites, corrupt desires and sensual delights (Gal. 5:16-21).

2. We **'fulfilled the desires of the flesh and mind'**. Desire here is the will and thoughts of our evil minds. Not only is our flesh corrupt, but also our affections, understanding and wills. We sinned because we willed to sin. We walked in darkness because we loved darkness (John 3:19).

3. The reason for all this: **'We were children of wrath by nature.'** This is the root or cause of our sin and miserable slavery. From our conception, birth and cradle we are children of wrath — God's wrath!

vv.4,5. **'But God who is rich in mercy . . .'** Mercy is an attribute of God as well as righteousness and justice. God's mercy is plenteous, free and infinite in Christ. His love and mercy to his chosen people in Christ are from everlasting and arise altogether out of himself, not because of any merit foreseen in them.

'Even when we were dead in sins,' he made us alive in union and fellowship with Christ. Consider this in two ways.

1. When our Lord lived on this earth, we lived in him. When he died, we died in him. When Christ arose and ascended, we arose and are now seated with him in the heavenlies. In this sense we are quickened with Christ.

2. In regeneration (the new birth) a sinner (dead spiritually) is made alive in Christ. He is given a new nature, a new heart and becomes a new creature. Christ is that life: for he is the author, the cause and the source of life (Col. 3:4). It is a gift of his grace.

vv.6,7. This is a spiritual resurrection from death (in sin and separation from God) unto spiritual life (a living union with God in Christ). Christ (our Representative, our federal Head, our great High Priest) has already entered into heaven, and we are loved, forgiven, accepted and made one with God in him.

Throughout eternity we shall be displayed as the trophies of God's wonderful grace. All of the elect angels and elect men will forever praise the Lord for his mercy and kindness toward us in Christ Jesus (Rev. 5:9-14).

vv.8, 9.   We are redeemed from death and sin to life and glory by the free grace of God. Election, redemption, calling, repentance, faith, sanctification and eternal glory are all ours by the free grace of our Lord (1 Cor. 1:30). Faith in Christ is the way, means, or instrument by which we receive and enjoy salvation; and this saving faith is not the product of man, but the gift of God. We receive salvation by faith and give all the glory to God. Any works of righteousness done by us are not ours, but are by the grace of God.

v.10.   However, lest (by commending God's grace as the cause, source and sustaining power in salvation and excluding works as making any contribution in our justification) the apostle should give the impression that works and a holy life are unnecessary, he adds, '**We are his workmanship, created in Christ Jesus unto good works.**' The spirit that lives in us is the spirit of love, joy, faith, humility and truth. Our calling is a 'holy calling'. Our Father is a 'merciful and holy Father'. Our walk is with him (Phil. 1:9-11; 1 Tim. 6:11).

No more strangers - but sons

Ephesians 2:11-22

In the preceding verses of this chapter Paul magnifies the riches of God's grace toward Jew and Gentile sinners. We all were dead in trespasses and sins. We all were children of wrath, following Satan and fulfilling our lusts and desires. But God quickened us together with Christ. Both Jew and Gentile have need to praise the grace of God (Rom. 3:19-24).

v.11. The Ephesians are called upon to remember and consider further (in order that God's grace and mercy to them might be magnified) that they were not only dead in sin, but were Gentile <u>dogs</u> — not of the covenant people Israel, not of the house of Abraham, not of the people to whom the promises, prophecies and sacrifices were given. They were called uncircumcised by way of reproach and contempt.

v.12. As Gentiles, **'Ye were without Christ.'** The Messiah was promised to Israel, the prophecies concerning the Saviour were given to Israel and the types, sacrifices and priesthood were of Israel.

'Aliens from the commonwealth of Israel.' So great an alienation and distance was there between Jew and Gentile that Gentiles could not dwell among Jews, eat nor converse with them, marry them, eat the Passover, nor join with them in worship.

'Strangers from the covenant of promise,' to the covenant given to Abraham, to the covenant at Sinai and to the covenant of grace. It might read, 'strangers to the promises of the covenant'.

'Having no hope' of a Messiah or salvation by him, no hope of the first resurrection or eternal life (Rev. 20:5,6).

'Without God in the world,' without any knowledge of God, without any prescribed worship of God, without any sacrifice or sin-offering by which to approach God. It was said, 'He who dwells outside the land of Israel is like one who has no God!'

v.13. But now, being chosen in Christ, redeemed in Christ, called to faith in Christ and becoming believers in Christ, we who were far from his law, his land, his people (aliens, strangers, without any knowledge of God) are made one with God through the blood of Christ. We are sons of God, having boldness to enter into the holiest by the blood of Christ (Heb. 10:19-22).

> Near, so near to God —
> Nearer I cannot be:
> For in the person of his Son,
> I am as near as he!

v.14. Christ is the author of peace with God, the giver of peace to our hearts and the maker of peace between Jew and Gentile. The wall may refer to the wall in the temple which divided the court of Israel from the court of the Gentiles and kept them at a distance in worship; but it definitely is the ceremonial law of circumcision, types and sacrifices, for Christ is the fulfilment of all for Jew and Gentile (Rom. 1:16,17).

v.15. Christ, in his flesh, abolished all differences between Jew and Gentile. He is the tabernacle, where God meets men and men meet God. He is the one great High Priest, who intercedes on behalf of all. He is the Passover, the Lamb of God, the atonement. Circumcision is of the heart (not in the flesh) and results in a broken heart toward sin and God. All believers are one (Gal. 6:15; 3:28).

v.16. By one body is meant either the human body of Christ, in which he obeyed the law, suffered for our sins, arose and ascended, or it may be meant that he reconciled all believers into one mystical body, the church of which he is the head. This he did by the cross, having slain the enmity of the law (both moral and ceremonial) (Eph. 5:22,23).

v.17. He came by his Spirit in the ministry of his apostles, preaching Christ, who is our peace (peace made by his blood) and the gospel of peace to Jew and Gentile.

v.18. Jew and Gentile have access to the Father through Christ. Neither the law nor justice stand in the way of a believing sinner approaching God if he comes through Christ alone (Heb. 4:14-16).

vv.19,20. Now we are no more aliens (strangers or foreigners) but citizens of the city of God, sons of God in his household. Christ is the foundation on which the church is built. He is the cornerstone which knits together all believers — Jew and Gentile, Old and New Testament saints, saints on earth and saints above, in all ages and places (Matt. 16:15-18; 1 Cor. 3:10,11).

vv.21,22. This is a spiritual building and will abide for ever. It is the church of the Lord Jesus Christ. It grows and is brought together as God calls out his elect. It is not finished yet as it will be. It is the habitation of God through the Spirit. God dwells in his people (1 Peter 2:4,5).

The mystery of Christ revealed

Ephesians 3:1-8

v.1. This epistle was written when Paul was a prisoner in Rome. He called himself 'the prisoner of Jesus Christ' because he was in prison for preaching Christ and his gospel. The only crime of which he was guilty was preaching the gospel of Christ and that to the Gentiles. He taught them that circumcision and the rest of the ceremonies of the law were not binding on them, that Christ is the end of the law for righteousness to all who believe. This stirred up the Jews against him and led to his imprisonment. 'Therefore I am a prisoner for the sake of you Gentiles.' Another thought to comfort is that the forces of evil only have power over God's people as the Lord permits them (and it always works our good and his glory) (Gen. 50:19,20; Rom. 8:28).

v.2. The word 'dispensation' is stewardship or administration. The apostle Paul acted by divine authority. He was a steward or appointed ambassador of the mysteries of God to the Gentiles (Acts 9:15; 22:14,15).

vv.3,4. The gospel of Christ is often called a 'mystery' (Eph. 1:9; 5:32; 6:19; Col. 1:25-27). The Trinity, the union of two natures in Christ, the whole doctrine of salvation by grace, the union of Christ and the believer are all mysteries which the natural man does not know, understand, nor love. They must be revealed by God's Spirit, even to Paul (1 Cor. 2:7-11; Gal. 1:11,12).

v.5. The mystery of Christ (his incarnation, imputed right-eousness, sacrifice, resurrection and intercession) certainly was not known nor understood by men in general; nor was it revealed to the prophets and men of God in the Old Testament as clearly and as plainly as it is now revealed to the apostles and to us. Some hints were given to Adam; and the gospel was preached to and by Noah, Abraham, Moses, David and Isaiah; but it lay hidden for the most part in types, shadows and prophecies. One thing we know — whatever they understood about his person and work, it was not to the extent that we know and understand by his Spirit (Luke 24:44-47).

v.6. This was especially not understood by the Old Testament prophets: that the Gentiles should be heirs of God and joint-heirs with Christ right along with the Jews — that the Gentiles should be one with them in the same body, under one and the same Head (Jesus Christ), partakers of the same grace, and enjoy the same privileges in Christ. Even the apostles had difficulty with this mystery (Gal. 2:11-16).

v.7. He is a true minister of the gospel who is made a minister (not by men, but by God), called of God to the work of the ministry and given the gifts and grace which are required to fulfil his responsibility. The true minister can use natural capacity, education and acquired learning; but the gift of interpreting the Scriptures, presenting the gospel of free grace, leading men in the true worship of God, and taking oversight of the church is a distinct thing from natural ability, human learning, or even internal grace; it is given by the effectual working of God's power.

v.8. 'This grace to know Christ, to understand the mysteries of redemption in Christ and to preach Christ is given to me. I am unworthy of this high honour, for I am less than the least of all the saints, the chief of sinners.' The greatest saints are generally the most humble. They have the lowest thoughts of their works and are the greatest admirers of the grace of God. The reason for their humility is an awareness of their sinful natures and a discovery of the love and grace of God to them in Christ Jesus. Their subject is now and will always be the 'unsearchable riches of Christ' (Rom. 12:3-5).

Holy treasure in earthen vessels

Ephesians 3:8-21

The apostle Paul was a very humble man. The choice servants of God are, generally speaking, the most humble. The reasons for their humility are that they are most aware of their own sinfulness, they have greater discoveries of God's love and grace in Christ and, being more sorely tried, they lean more completely on the arm of grace.

v.8.   Paul saw great grace in being trusted with the ministry of the gospel and having such treasure put in an earthen vessel. He was appointed to take the gospel of Christ to the Gentiles.

v.9.   The mystery mentioned in this verse is the gospel of Christ (Mark 4:11; 1 Cor. 2:7,8). Natural men do not understand the gospel of substitution, do not see the wisdom of the cross and therefore must be born again, regenerated and taught of God (John 3:3; 6:44,45). The ministry of the Word is the means God uses to enlighten men (Rom. 10:13-15). The gospel was there from the beginning in the counsel and covenant of God; for he created all things in, by and for Christ (Col. 1:14-17); but it was hidden in some measure from the elect angels, from even the Old Testament saints and altogether from natural men.

v.10.   The purpose is that through and by the church of the Lord Jesus Christ the complex, many-sided wisdom of God in justifying the ungodly by Christ Jesus might be made known to the angels and powers even in heaven (1 Peter 1:12). The angels are witnesses of God's mercy to the church in Christ (Heb. 1:14).

v.11.   All of the salvation of sinners in Christ (which displays the wisdom and mercy of God) is according to his own eternal purpose, which he purposed in Christ before the world began. Christ the Redeemer and the time of his incarnation, sufferings and resurrection were all decreed by God (Acts 4:26-28). The persons for whom he became incarnate, suffered and died were chosen in him (Eph. 1:3-5).

v.12.   Therefore, because we are redeemed by Christ, our Representative (Rom. 5:19; 1 Cor. 15:21,22) and Substitute, and God has enabled us to believe on Christ (who is the object of saving faith), we have boldness to enter into the very presence of God with courage and confidence (Heb. 10:19-22).

v.13.   'So I ask you not to be discouraged because of the trials and troubles I have gone through to preach the gospel to you. I am not ashamed to be identified with Christ in reproach (Heb. 13:13) and hatred (John 15:18,19). It is an honour to be counted worthy to suffer with him (Heb. 11:24-26; 2 Cor. 1:6).

v.14.   **'For this cause I bow my knees unto the Father.'** The awesome responsibility of ministering the gospel, the privilege of access to the throne of grace and the perseverance of the believers in Ephesus led Paul to pray for them (2 Cor. 2:14-16; 3:5).

v.15.   He is the Father of all believers, all the elect in heaven and earth (John 1:12; 20:17).

vv.16-19.   This is the prayer Paul prayed for them:
    1. That God would strengthen them so that they would not faint under trial. That the Holy Spirit would strengthen their spirits, their hearts and their inner selves with fresh supplies of grace. Strength to live for God's glory is from within (John 7:37-39).
    2. This is the true source of all spiritual life, the key to union with the Father, the fountainhead of all blessings and the hope of eternal life — 'Christ in you' (Gal. 4:19; Col. 1:27).

That they might be rooted and grounded deep in love for Christ. This is our security — his love for us and our love for him.

3. That they might be able, with all believers, to have a greater understanding of the great love of God for us — what is the breadth, the length, the height and the depth of his love (Rom. 5:8).

4. That they might understand more of the special and peculiar love of Christ for his church, which is beyond perfect knowledge (his engaging to be Surety for them, his assumption of their nature, his payment for their debts, his giving them a perfect righteousness, his intercession, his constant supply of mercy and grace). We have some knowledge of it, but the more of it we know, the more we will be filled and flooded with Christ himself.

vv.20, 21. The prayer closes with a celebration of the perfection, power and glory of God. God begins, carries on and finishes the work he purposed to do for his people. This work of eternal redemption will be infinitely beyond our highest prayers, desires, thoughts, hopes, or dreams.

A walk worthy of our calling

Ephesians 4:1-7

In the first three chapters of this epistle Paul deals with the doctrines of the grace of God, explaining and establishing them. In the last three chapters he deals mainly with the duties of believers with regard to the Christian walk.

v.1. 'I beseech you to take heed to your conduct and conversation that your behaviour be a credit to him who by his grace called you out of darkness into his kingdom of light. In your attitude, speech, home life, business dealings and social contacts, conduct yourselves in a way that is becoming to the name of Christ which you wear. Adorn the gospel of Christ with righteousness' (Titus 2:7-10).

v.2.   **'In lowliness and meekness**,' that is, in the exercise of humility having the best thoughts of others and the lowest thoughts of ourselves; in not envying the gifts and graces of others but rejoicing in them; and in willingness to receive correction, rebuke and instruction.

'With long-suffering,' bearing patiently the faults and infirmities of others, not being easily provoked to anger nor being offended by slight or misunderstanding. God is certainly patient with us! (Gal. 6:1,2).

'Forbearing one another in love,' making whatever allowances are necessary because you love one another! (1 Cor. 13:4-7; 1 Peter 4:8).

v.3.   'Be eager and strive earnestly to protect and keep the harmony and oneness of spirit in the church.' This spiritual union between Christ and his people and between believers is produced by the Holy Spirit. We are united in faith, love, purpose and one body. My responsibility is to do all within my power to protect and preserve that unity, even to surrendering my rights and opinions (Ps. 133:1; 1 Cor. 3:1-3).

v.4.   **'There is one body**,' the church. It is called one body with respect to Jew and Gentile, to saints above and below and to separate classes and societies; for though there are several congregations and local churches, there is one church of which Christ is the Head and we are all brethren (Eph. 5:23; Col. 1:18).

'There is **one Spirit**,' the Holy Spirit of God, who enlightens, quickens, makes alive and incorporates us all in the body of Christ — members one of another.

'There is **one hope of your calling**,' that is, the glory hoped for and which is reserved for us in heaven. There are no degrees in this glory. It will be equally possessed by all; for they are all loved with the same love, chosen in the same Head, redeemed by the same blood and secured in the same covenant.

v.5. **'One Lord,'** the Lord Jesus Christ, who is Lord by right of creation (Col. 1:16,17), of the Father's decree (Acts 2:36) and of his sacrificial death (Rom. 14:9; Phil. 2:9-11).

'One faith.' There is but one true grace of faith. It may be little faith, much faith, or great faith; but its author and object are the same in all — the Lord Jesus Christ in his person and work (John 3:36).

'One baptism.' There is one baptism under the gospel, which is water baptism; to be administered in one and the same way — by immersion; with one and the same subjects — believers; and in the name of the Father, Son and Holy Spirit (Matt. 28:19; Acts 8:36-39).

v.6. There is one eternal, infinite, omnipotent God of heaven and earth, who is the Father of all believers in Christ and who is sovereign over all, taking care of us all and dwelling in us all. Paul is saying (in vv. 4-6) that, as believers, we have all these things in common — one body, one Spirit, one hope, one Lord, one faith, one baptism, one God, who is our Father. Therefore, we must and will be one family joined together in love stronger than anything this world can know. To disturb that unity is displeasing to God (Prov. 6:16-19).

v.7. God's grace was given to us individually — grace to know Christ, to walk with Christ and to minister for the glory of Christ. He gives grace and gifts as he will and to whom he will, and there is no room for pride, envy, or contempt (1 Cor. 4:7).

The work of the ministry

Ephesians 4:8-16

v.8. This is a quotation from Psalm 68:18, and it speaks of our Lord's ascension to heaven from Mt Olivet in the sight of the apostles (Acts 1:9-11). In this he fulfils the type of the High Priest entering into the holiest to make intercession for

his people, to prepare a place for them and to send down the
Holy Spirit with his grace and gifts to them.

'He led captivity captive.' He led a train of vanquished foes;
he conquered those who had conquered us, such as sin, Satan
and death. Christ conquered and triumphed over every spiritual
enemy and those of his people.

'And gave gifts to men' — the gifts of the Holy Spirit, and
especially such as qualify men for the work of the ministry
and make them useful for God's glory and the good of the
church (Rom. 12:5-8).

vv.9,10.   These verses are simply saying that it could not be
said of Christ that he ascended into heaven if he had not first
descended or come down to the earth (John 3:13). 'The lower
parts of the earth' does not mean hell (as the Catholics say),
but rather the whole of his humiliation, beginning with his
mother's womb. He was made flesh!

'That he might fulfil all things' that were written, prophesied
and typified of him. All that he did, is doing and will do is
according to the Scriptures (1 Cor. 15:3,4; Luke 24:27).

v.11.   He himself appointed and gave men gifts that qualified
them to be **apostles**. This was the first and chief office in the
church. They were called by Christ, had their doctrine directly
from him and had a power to work miracles to confirm their
doctrine (Heb. 2:3,4). This office is now ceased.

'And some prophets' — not ordinary ministers of the Word
but unusual men of God in the early church who had a particular gift to interpret Scripture (especially the prophecies of
the Old Testament) and of foretelling things to come, such as
Agabus (Acts 11:27-30).

'Evangelists' — preachers of the gospel who were travelling
missionaries.

'Pastors and teachers.' Many say this is one and the same
office, and it may be, for every true pastor is a teacher of the
Scriptures. But it seems to me that there are teachers in the
church who are not pastors. Pastors are the shepherds of the
flock, while teachers may be gifted brethren in the church,
teachers of the Word and assistants to the pastors.

v.12.   The reason Christ gave us these ministers of the gospel
is for **'the perfecting of all believers'**, for the best of believers
are imperfect. Our faith, love, knowledge and sanctification
need growth and maturity (1 Peter 2:2).

   'For the work of the ministry,' to preach the gospel to the
lost (2 Tim. 2:10), to oversee the church (1 Peter 5:1-4) and
to teach the things of Christ (Matt. 28:19,20).

   'For the edifying of the body of Christ.' We preach and
teach, not to divide nor to scatter the sheep, but to strengthen,
build up and give comfort and assurance to the people of God.

v.13.   We pray, preach and teach until all the elect come to
saving faith and are united in their sentiments concerning
Christ, the source and object of faith. We preach until all of
the elect come to a spiritual knowledge of Christ, behold his
glory, trust in him and appropriate him to themselves. We
preach that the elect may grow to a spiritual maturity. We will
not be perfect until Christ comes and we are conformed to his
image; but we, through proper use of the Word, grow from
spiritual infancy to maturity and strength in Christ (1 Peter
2:1,2). The next two verses indicate that this is the meaning.

vv.14,15.   When we were first converted, we were babes in
Christ — babes in understanding, having to be fed with milk;
babes in strength, having to be protected, watched over and
pacified; babes in fruit, having the buds of the fruit of the
Spirit but not the full flower. As children we are in danger
from false teachers, cunning men and strange doctrines. As our
true ministers feed us the Word of God, we grow up in all
things in Christ. We become strong in faith, love, patience,
knowledge and all grace. The danger of our being deceived or
led away from Christ is lessened. The Word of truth is the
instrumental means of such growth (1 John 2:12,13).

v.16.   Because of Christ, who is our Head, the whole church
(called the whole body) in its various parts and members is
joined and firmly knit together (1 Cor. 12:12,13,27). The
bond (or cement) which holds us together is the grace of faith
and love supplied by Christ to every part. When each part or

member is working properly, the body grows to full maturity
and builds itself up in love.

Put off the old man and put on the new

Ephesians 4:17-32

v.17.   Before conversion, believers walk as others (Eph.
2:2,3). But when we are brought to a knowledge of Christ,
our walk, conduct and conversation are not (or ought not be)
like the unconverted. **'The vanity of the mind'** is vain philosophy, foolish thoughts of self and God, the pursuit of worldly
riches, honour and acclaim, and the continued effort to find
pleasure and happiness in the world (Ps. 39:5).

vv.18,19.   The unbelieving Gentiles are intelligent and wise
enough in evil things, but in spiritual things their understanding
is darkened (2 Cor. 4:3,4; 1 Cor. 2:7-9).
     They are alienated from the life of God because of sin.
They have natural life and knowledge, but have no spiritual
life nor proper knowledge of God (John 8:19, 42-44).
     They are ignorant and their hearts are hardened against God.
Every natural man is ignorant of spiritual things and his heart
is hardened daily by sin (Rom. 8:7).
     In their ignorance, deadness and carnality, they have given
themselves to sensuality, eager to indulge in every form of evil
and dishonesty. They are given to whatever sin their corrupt
natures may suggest or desire.

v.20.   Believers cannot live in this manner, for a life of sin
and indulgence in fleshly carnality is certainly not the life of
Christ as we have been taught by his Spirit.

vv.21,22.   'Assuming that the Lord has spoken to you
through his Word and by his Spirit and that you have been
taught the truth as it is in Christ Jesus (John 6:44,45), you

will put off and discard your old way of life. You will deny
the old man (the old nature) the right to rule over you. The
old nature has its lusts and desires, but they are deceitful.
They promise pleasure and profit but yield neither! Put down
this old nature with strong denials' (1 Tim. 6:11; Titus 2:11,12).

v.23. By prayer, worship, reading the Word and continued
feeding upon Christ, our spiritual man is refreshed, revived and
renewed (Ps. 51:10)

v.24. To **'put on'** the new nature is not to make ourselves
new creatures in Christ, for this is God's work and not man's.
It is God who regenerates and creates a new man in true
righteousness and holiness. But to **'put on the new man'** is to
walk daily according to the principles of grace and holiness
formed in us. Walk in the spirit of Christ and avoid not only the
works of evil but the very appearance of evil (1 Thess. 5:22).

v.25. Reject and denounce lying, exaggeration and any
effort to deceive. Speak tactfully and kindly words of truth to
one another; for we are of the same body and a man is foolish
to lie to himself.

vv.26,27. There is an anger which is not sinful, for anger is
found in God and in Christ! It arises from a true zeal for God
and for holiness and it is not against persons but against sins.
But do not allow even this anger to continue: let it be over
when the day is over. All anger and indignation should quickly
be forgotten (James 1:19,20). Do not give Satan any room,
foothold, or opportunity to use you for evil purposes or to
hinder the kingdom of God by your anger and bad attitude.

v.28. Stealing takes many directions — actual theft, obtaining
possessions by false representation, failing to pay debts and
receiving wages while not putting forth our best efforts. Make
an honest living and be able and willing to share with others.

v.29. Let your conversation be seasoned with grace and
language which is spiritually beneficial to others. Avoid

unwholesome words, worthless talk, gossip and excessive levity
(Col. 3:8,9; 4:6).

v.30.   The things mentioned above grieve, vex and offend the
Holy Spirit of God, who dwells in us and by whom we are
sealed unto the day of final redemption.

v.31.   Let all bitterness and wrath (bad temper, resentment
and rage) be put away. Let all contention, strife and quarrelling,
along with all slander and ill will, be put away! (Col. 3:19.)

v.32.   Become useful, helpful, kind and tender-hearted with
one another; and forgive one another readily and freely as God
in Christ forgave you (Matt. 6:14,15).

Be ye followers of God as his children

Ephesians 5:1-17

v.1.   The opening sentence gives us the theme of this chapter.
As the children of God, we are to imitate and follow after him
in acts of righteousness and holiness, in loving and forgiving
one another, in acts of mercy and goodness and in freely
distributing to the needs of others (Titus 2:7-10).

v.2.   'Walk in love.' Here is the key to all that is commanded,
expected and needed for godliness and sanctification! (1) Live
in love to God our Father, who has given us all things in Christ;
(2) live in love to Christ, for the love he has for us, the relationship we have with him and the things he has done for us,
but chiefly (3) live in love to one another. Our example is
Christ, who loved us and give himself for us. He was both
Priest and Sacrifice, giving his blood as a sacrifice to redeem us
to God. This principle of love is sufficient motivation for
mercy, forgiveness, kindness and all godliness! (Matt. 22:36-40;
John 13:34,35; 1 John 3:23.)

vv.3,4. Paul names several sinful practices which are unbecoming to children of God and which love for Christ and for one another should constrain them to avoid. **'Fornication'** is committed between unmarried persons and was thought by the Gentiles not to be sinful. **'Uncleanness'** includes adultery, incest, homosexuality and all unnatural lusts. **'Covetousness'** is an immoderate desire after worldly, material things, but, judging from the context, it denotes continual thoughts and desires for the above lusts. Not only should believers avoid these sins, but they should avoid any thoughts or suggestions by liberal thinkers that they are not exceedingly sinful!

'Filthiness, foolish talking' and **'jesting'** are sins of the mouth and tongue. It is much more becoming for a believer to be giving thanks to God and speaking of his kingdom, his mercy and his blessings than to employ his tongue in secular foolishness. To be more precise, filthiness of tongue is obscene words, blasphemy and offensive language. Foolish talking is vain, idle and unprofitable babbling, filled with exaggeration and worldliness. Jesting can become sinful when too much emphasis is given to humour, kidding and joking. Christians are happy people. They are a family of joyful friends who can share humour, experiences and pleasures; but they must carefully avoid even wholesome humour, giving themselves to more spiritual conversation which edifies and builds up the believer in faith.

vv.5-7. 'With reference to fornication, unclean sexual practices and greed for the material things of this world (which is really idolatry), don't be deceived by the vain words of so-called free thinkers and liberal religionists. These practices are evil, and no person who walks in this manner has any inheritance in the kingdom of God. A sinful, corrupt life brings the wrath of God upon a religious person as quickly as upon an atheist. Do not be a partaker with the evil men even though they profess to believe on Christ.'

v.8. 'At one time you were in total darkness, not knowing the evil of sin, the will of God, nor his true righteousness. You gave vent to the flesh and cared not for the glory of God. You

are no longer in darkness, but are enlightened by the Spirit of
God. Therefore, walk as children of light, not in sin and the
works of darkness, but in faith, truth and holiness.'

v.9.   The fruit of the Spirit (the kind of life produced by the
presence of the Holy Spirit) is '**goodness**' (as opposed to greed,
lust and cruelty), '**righteousness**' (as opposed to carnality, evil
and worldliness) and '**truth**' (as opposed to hypocrisy, lying
and deceit). Where the Spirit of God dwells, there will be to
some degree the appearance of this fruit (Gal. 5:22).

v.10.   There are many things which are '**acceptable to the
Lord**' − the person of Christ, his righteousness, sacrifice and
mediation, the persons of his people in Christ and the lives and
conversation of his people when they are becoming to the
gospel and according to his will (Col. 3:20; Heb. 13:15,16,
20,21).

v.11.   The believer will not and cannot find and enjoy social
fellowship with ungodly and profane people (2 Cor. 6:14-18).
Though we must work, live as neighbours and often converse
with unbelievers, it is impossible for a true believer to enjoy
and seek out the company of persons who know not and do
not love our Lord. We reprove them not only with words but
with a godly life which exposes their vain way of life, as light
that drives away darkness (Heb. 11:7).

vv.12,13.   Their secret lives of pride, lust, envy, hate and
idolatry are even shameful to speak about; but as light reveals
and discovers things unseen in darkness, so the sins and evil of
men will be discovered and revealed by a true witness of the
gospel of Christ and a godly life and attitude. All righteousness
(whether by word or deed) which reveals sins is considered
spiritual light.

vv.14-17.   This is written to the believer; for the children of
God sometimes need to be revived, awakened and rebuked for
their indifference and carelessness (Rom. 13:11-14). 'Take
heed to your walk. Don't be a fool; the fashion of this world

passes away. See to your calling and election; examine your faith; take inventory of your worship, prayer and devotional life; look to your attitude and daily walk.' Wise men walk with God in a careful and diligent use of the time God has given them because these are evil days and many are led away. 'Do not be unwise, but seek the will of the Lord!'

Obedience - authority and love

Ephesians 5:18-33

v.18. Drunkenness is the excessive drinking of any strong drink, and it is strongly condemned in the Scriptures. Wine is mentioned here because it was the usual liquor people drank in these Eastern countries. Excessive drinking deprives a person of reason, hurts the mind, brings disease to the body, opens the door to every sin, wastes possessions and sets a man below the beasts. **'Be filled with the Holy Spirit.'** People with the Holy Spirit have spiritual joy and are controlled and dominated by the Spirit, as wine controls and dominates the drunkard. Their walk, talk and thinking are all influenced by the Spirit.

v.19. **'Speaking to yourselves in psalms, hymns and spiritual songs.'** When the Holy Spirit dwells within us like a well of living water and our hearts dwell on the goodness and mercy of God, the melodies and tunes with which we cheer ourselves and others are not the profane, loose and carnal songs of flesh, but are songs consisting of spirituality which gladden the heart and edify the soul (Col. 3:16).

v.20. **'Giving thanks always for all things'** (James 1:17; John 3:27). All mercies, temporal and spritual, come from the Father through our Lord Jesus; and for these mercies in Christ we continually praise and thank God (1 Thess. 5:18). We give thanks for electing love, redeeming grace, eternal life, Christian fellowship, food, affliction and trials and all things (Rom. 8:28).

Murmuring and complaining against the providence of God is a great sin.

v.21. 'Submitting yourselves to one another.' Christ is the sovereign Head of the church, the supreme authority and King of the saints; and as such he is to be feared and reverenced. He delegates authority in his name in the home, in the church and in the world. In fear of the Lord and in reverence for him and his glory, we submit ourselves to that authority — as wives to husbands, children to parents, servants to masters, members of the church to pastors and all men to civil magistrates (Rom. 13:1-4).

v.22. 'Wives, submit yourselves to your own husbands.' This subjection is not only in body, but in heart and spirit! Wives should think well of husbands, speak respectfully of them and to them, take care of family matters according to their husbands' will, imitate them in that which is good and bear patiently that which is not so agreeable. 'As unto the Lord,' because the Lord has commanded it, because the husband is the Lord's authority in the home and because rebellion against designated spiritual authority is rebellion against the Lord.

vv.23,24. Pertaining to redemption, in Christ there is neither male nor female, bond nor free; but Christ is all. But in the divine order governing the family of God on earth, our Lord has decreed authority and leadership which is to be obeyed and followed (1 Cor. 11:3; 1 Tim. 2:11-15).

Therefore, as the church is dependent on Christ, resigned to him, receiving from him protection, provision, comfort and happiness in a voluntary, sincere and hearty obedience (arising from a principle of love), so let the wives be subject to their husbands in things political, domestic and ecclesiastic.

v.25. 'Husbands, love your wives.' This is still and always will be the key to any relationship! Because Christ loved us, he gave himself for us; because we love Christ, his yoke is easy and his burden is light. If a husband loves his wife as Christ loved the church (showing affection for her, delighting in her, seeking her contentment and happiness, concealing her faults, preferring her above his parents, neighbours or children and properly leading her in things spiritual), her submission will be a delight and joy to her.

vv.26,27. Because of the context, this reference seems to be to the custom of the Jews in their engagements to marry. A man was engaged to be married to a woman provided she had no spots, blemishes, nor past sexual affairs. If afterwards these faults were found in her, the marriage was off. But Christ found us guilty, sinful and full of fault. He loved us and cleansed us in his own blood so that he might present us holy and without spot in that day.

vv.28-30. Men ought to love their wives as they love themselves, for the two are actually one flesh (Gen. 2:23-25). The Lord and his church are one. This is the church of the first-born, composed of every true believer of every generation.

v.31. A man does not desert nor disown his parents; but he loves, cares and shows respect for them, honouring them as long as they live. But his marriage is the establishment of a new home and a new family, which his parents are not to interfere with nor try to control. His wife is to be preferred before his parents, and she is not to be allowed to suffer at their hands, nor are they to be allowed to come between husband and wife.

vv.32,33. The marriage union is compared to Christ's union with his church. He left his Father's house to come to earth. He loved us with infinite affection. He and his church are one. He provides for us, protects us and gives us his name for ever. We love and are in subjection to him!

Everyday theology

Ephesians 6:1-10

I will divide this portion of the chapter into five parts:
1. The duties of children to parents;
2. The duties of parents to children;
3. The duties of servants to masters;
4. The duties of masters to servants;
5. Exhortation to all believers.

I *vv. 1-3.*   This verse refers mainly to unmarried children who are yet living at home with their parents. There is an honour, respect and reverence that is due to our parents all the days of our lives. Children at home are under the authority of parents as God's ministers and representatives, and they are to be respected and obeyed with a sincere and willing obedience as if their words and wishes were the words of God himself. Of course, '**in the Lord**' would rule out obeying our parents in evil activities which are contrary to the Word of God.

This honouring of our parents touches several areas. It goes beyond loving them, obeying their commands, overlooking their infirmities and speaking respectfully of and to them. They are to be honoured in our thoughts and attitudes. They are to be cared for in their old age. This is the first commandment that carries with it a promise (as indicated in v.3 and Exod. 20:12).

II *v.4.*   Fathers are named because they are the heads of the families and are apt to be too severe (mothers are sometimes too indulgent); but both parents are intended, for both are responsible for the general welfare and behaviour of the children. Children can be alienated from parents, from Christian doctrine and from the church by unwise and unreasonable discipline. 'Spare the rod and spoil the child' does not mean that children are to be beaten. The rod of discipline can be exercised in other and more effectual ways. Public rebuke, harsh language and passionate rages and tantrums are to be avoided. Refusing them proper recreation and wholesome fellowship with other children will discourage them. They are not adults and should not be expected to think, behave, nor even to reason like adults. Adult problems and misunderstandings, especially church difficulties, should never be discussed in the presence of children. They should be protected as much as possible from the trials of a difficult world until they are more mature.

III   *vv.5-8.*   Servants or workers, be obedient to those who are your superiors in things pertaining to the flesh. If you work for a person or you are under a foreman or a boss, do what you are told to do, do what you are paid to do, do what you are hired to do without complaining and quarrelling, but with respect and humility. Serve your superiors in singleness of heart, that is, cheerfully, readily and with full effort, as if you were serving Christ himself, for all of our deeds are to be done for the glory of Christ.

There are some workers who pretend to work with great diligence and industry when the boss is present (in order to impress him); then when no one is watching, they loaf and neglect their work. This is evil! We should work as diligently in his absence as in his presence; for believers have an eye to pleasing and glorifying God, not just winning the approval of men.

Working with '**good will . . . as to the Lord**' is working with a good attitude, going beyond what we are told or expected to do, thankful that we have the health to work and a job with which to support our families and with concern for our superior's business and success.

Know this: that whatever a man does out of a right motive and principle of his heart for the glory of Christ, he will be blessed of God, whether he is a master or a servant!

IV   *v.9.*   Masters, bosses and superiors, perform the duties and responsibilities toward your work as you would have your

servants do theirs (the same way, with charity and humanity,
as unto the Lord). Treat your servants as you would be treated.
Pay them well, speak firmly but respectfully to them, remembering that you have a Master in heaven who deals with men as
they deal with others. Your riches, power and position mean
nothing to him; for he gives to all men the strength and
possessions they have (1 Sam. 2:6,7). A good master is as
difficult to find as a good servant.

V   *v.10.*   This begins the conclusion of Paul's exhortation
on the duties of believers to others. He addresses them all and
says, '**Finally, brethren, be strong in the Lord**.'
    1. The things which are commanded are impossible to
perform without God's strength and grace.
    2. We need his strength and power to overcome our enemies,
our flesh and Satan. We need his strength to adorn the doctrine
of Christ with holiness and integrity.
    3. Though we are weak and can do nothing of ourselves, his
grace is sufficient for all things.

The whole armour of God

Ephesians 6:11-24

v.11.   The believer lives in a world of evil. He is surrounded
by evil powers and evil people. This world is not the friend of
grace nor of God. Not only is sin around us, but sin is within
us. The Christian life is a race to be run (Heb. 12:1), a battle
to be fought (1 Tim. 6:12; 2 Tim. 4:7) and a conflict that will
not be over until we die. We need help and strength to stand
up against all of the deceit and strategies of Satan, who is the
great enemy of Christ and his people. God has provided an
armour for his people and weapons to be used against Satan,
sin and error.

v.12.   We are not contending against physical opponents.

Frail, mortal men are not our real enemies. Our battle is against wicked spirits, who inhabit the supernatural sphere and who deal in lies, pride, idolatry, covetousness, lust, deceit, self-righteousness and all manner of sin against God.

v.13. 'Take upon yourselves the complete armour that God has provided for you, that you may be able to resist these evils and stand during every trial, conflict and temptation and having met every demand to continue to stand firmly in Christ.' The battle is not against the flesh; therefore, the armour and weapons which God provides are not carnal but spiritual (2 Cor. 10:3-5).

vv.14-18. The parts of this armour are given in these verses.
   1. '**Your loins girt about with truth.** Wrap about you (as a strong girdle) the gospel of God's redemptive glory in and through Christ Jesus' (1 Peter 1:13). This is the first part of the armour mentioned, for it is the most important and the foundation of all the rest. The truth about God, myself and my race and Christ and his redemptive work keeps me close to God and defends me against all evil suggestions of Satan which lead to a false hope.
   2. '**The breastplate of righteousness.**' This breastplate of integrity, right standing before God and holiness cannot be works of righteousness and moral integrity done and produced by me, for Satan could easily find a defect in that breastplate and destroy me. But this is the righteousness of Christ, my Lord. His perfect righteousness imputed to me and received by faith repels any accusation or charge which Satan can bring (Rom. 8:33,34).
   3. '**Your feet shod with the preparation of the gospel of peace.**' Several things could be taught here: a firm-footed stability or foundation in the gospel of peace; a godly walk that is agreeable to the gospel of peace; a readiness to go forth into the highways and hedges declaring the good news of peace through Christ.
   4. '**Take the shield of faith.**' Satan hurls darts of doubt, fear, depression, weariness and all manner of questions regarding our spiritual state. We can only be shielded against these fiery

darts by faith in God's Word (Rom. 4:20,21), faith in God's
purpose (Rom. 8:29,30) and faith in Christ's redeeming work
(Rom. 8:34-39).

5. 'Take the helmet of salvation.' The helmet is a piece of
armour for the head and protects the head against false doctrines. This helmet is the hope of salvation in Christ alone —
the salvation of which Christ is the author and the finisher
(1 Thess. 5:8,9; 1 Cor. 1:30).

6. 'The sword of the Spirit, which is the word of God.' The
Word of God is compared to a sword in that it has two edges
— the law and the gospel (Heb. 4:12). It is all edge; it has no
blunt side. One cannot come near the Word without its having
some effect. It convicts of sin, cutting away the righteousness
of men; it kills pride, envy, lusts and all sin; it reaches the
hidden and secret parts; it is the weapon God uses to defeat all
his enemies (Luke 4:3-12).

7. 'Praying.' The last weapon is prayer and includes all sorts
of prayer — mental, vocal, private and public. We should live in
an attitude of prayer continually. Our prayers must and will be
in the Spirit, by the assistance of the Spirit of God, with a
sincere heart for all believers. We will persevere in prayer
regardless of the suggestions of Satan or our own weak hearts.

v.19.   Pray for the ministers of the gospel, that God will not
only open effectual doors for them to preach, but that he will
give them boldness and wisdom to preach the gospel of Christ
(which is a mystery only understood as the Holy Spirit reveals
it — 1 Cor. 2:8-10; Rom. 10:13-17).

v.20.   Paul called himself an ambassador of Christ (2 Cor.
5:19,20). He was at that time in prison.

vv.21,22.   Tychicus was a beloved brother, who accompanied
Paul on his travels, whom Paul sent to the Ephesians to relate
to them Paul's affairs and to encourage them in the gospel.

vv.23,24.   The epistle is concluded with the apostle's salutation. Those saluted are the brethren who love Christ sincerely.
He wishes for them peace, love, faith and grace.

Philippians

A letter from Paul to the Philippians

Phillippians 1:1-11

Introduction. Philippi was a Roman colony and the chief city of Macedonia. Paul had received special instructions to go there (Acts 16:9-12). Lydia and the jailer (as well as others) were converted, forming the church at Philippi.

Paul was in prison at Rome when he wrote this epistle. He mentions his chains, Caesar's palace and some of Caesar's household sending their greetings to the church.

Paul was especially dear to these Philippians. He was the preacher who had brought them the gospel. Upon hearing that he was a prisoner in Rome, they sent their minister, Epaphroditus, to him with presents and good wishes. He sent this epistle back to them by their minister.

The design of the epistle is:

1. To express his love and affection for them.

2. To give an account of his imprisonment and the results of it.

3. To encourage them under affliction and persecution.

4. To excite them to love, unity and peace among themselves.

5. To caution them against false teachers, who were trying to mix Moses and Christ, the law and the gospel, grace and works in salvation.

6. To exhort them to a holy life and behaviour.

7. To give thanks to them for their care for him.

v.1. Paul, though the sole writer of this epistle, includes Timothy in his salutation for several reasons.

1. Timothy was with Paul when he preached in Philippi.

2. He planned to send Timothy to them (Phil. 2:19-23).

3. He shows the continued agreement between them in love and doctrine: **'The servants (bondslaves) of Jesus Christ.'** Paul

does not say, 'I am an apostle, and Timothy is young and less important.' He chooses a character which fits them both — willing, loving bondslaves of Christ. (See Exod. 21:2-6.)

'**To all the saints, bishops and deacons at Philippi.**' Every believer is a saint, consecrated and sanctified in Christ. The bishops are the pastors and elders, concerned mainly with the spiritual state of the members. The deacons (along with the spiritual concern) are the servants of the church, who serve the Lord's Table, the tables of the poor and the secular affairs of the church.

vv.2-5.   This is a prayer of thanksgiving and petition.

1. He prays for grace and peace to be in them and upon them (v.2).

2. He thanks God for every thought and memory of them (v.3).

3. His memory of them and prayers for them bring him great joy (v.4).

4. He thanks God for their fellowship in the gospel from the first day until now (v.5). This is the attitude we need to cultivate toward other believers. Leave off judging, criticizing and finding fault. Not only thank God for one another, but pray for his grace and peace to be with all believers.

> May he by whose kind grace we meet,
> Send his great Spirit from above,
> Make our communications sweet,
> And cause our hearts to burn with love.

v.6.   Paul's thanksgiving and joy on behalf of this church sprang from the confidence and persuasion that the work of grace which God had begun in them would result in their eternal glorification with Christ.

1. The '**good work**' is regeneration, conversion, salvation and the forming of Christ in them.

2. It is '**begun**'. It is not yet finished. We are saved, we are being saved and we will finally be saved when we awake with his likeness.

3. It is a work '**in you**'. Christ does a work *for* us and also a work *in* us, sanctifying and making us new creatures (Eph. 2:8-10).

4. *He* does the work. He is the author and finisher of our faith. Salvation is of the Lord from beginning to end (1 Cor. 4:7).

vv. 7, 8. Paul further justifies his confidence in regard to these people on the basis of two other reasons: Firstly, God kept them on Paul's heart continually, and, secondly, they stood by him in love and defence of the gospel.

'It is right and appropriate for me to have this confidence and feel this way about you all, because even as you do me, I hold you in my heart as partakers and sharers, one and all with me, of grace. This is true when I am shut up in prison and when I am out in the field — for God is my witness how I long for and pursue you all with love' (Amplified Version).

vv. 9-11. Paul again prays for them.

1. 'That your love may overflow more and more.' Growth in grace includes growth in the grace of love for Christ and his people.

2. 'That your love may increase **in knowledge and judgement.**' Our love for Christ and his people is not blind, ignorant infatuation. We know him, and the more we know of him in his perfection, the more we love him. We know them — frail, weak and human like ourselves; yet our love grows as we are able to judge and discern true spiritual values.

3. '**That you may approve things that are excellent.**' Or, 'that you may learn to sense what is of real value and excellence.' There is a difference in self-love and Christian love, in religious works and works of faith, and in knowing the doctrine of Christ and the Christ of doctrine.

4. '**That you may be sincere** in your desires after God,' not stumbling nor causing others to stumble.

5. 'That you may be **filled with the fruits of righteousness,**' right standing before God in Christ and right doing for the glory of Christ!

Encouragement during trial

Philippians 1:12-30

The church at Philippi had heard of the apostle's troubles. He
wanted them to have a true and right understanding of trials
and afflictions. He desired that the weak among them might
not be offended and that all among them might be encouraged
to bear with patience and cheerfulness whatever afflictions
might befall them for Christ's sake.

vv.12,13. 'Now, I want you to understand and rest assured
that my imprisonment has actually served to advance and give
renewed strength to the spreading of the gospel.' Persecution
for Christ's sake has often meant the carrying of the gospel to
other places (Acts 8:4; 11:19,20). Someone said, 'The blood
of martyrs is the seed of the church.' Also, persecution (our
behaviour under it and our attitude toward it) attracts attention
and encourages others (Matt. 5:16).

Paul was not in prison for breaking the law, but for preaching the gospel of Christ (Acts 24:10-14). This was generally
known throughout Caesar's court and in all other places. The
gospel, as a result of Paul's confinement, had become an issue
throughout the court (Acts 26:26). Our discomfort may be
used of God to bring eternal comfort to others. It is said that
ancient believers sold themselves into slavery to preach to the
slaves. 'Christ became poor that we through his poverty might
be rich' (2 Tim. 2:9,10).

v.14. Paul's sufferings not only resulted in the conversion of
many outside the church, but were encouraging and strengthen-
ing to many within the church. These brethren were challenged
and encouraged by Paul's patience and faithfulness under
suffering. Many became bold to declare the gospel of Christ.
Our attitude and our general conduct during trials have a strong

influence one way or the other upon those who watch us.

vv.15-17. I believe we can safely say that, whoever these men were, they truly preached the gospel of God's redeeming grace in Christ. Otherwise, Paul would not have rejoiced in their ministry (Gal. 1:8).

1. Some preached Christ out of *envy*. They envied Paul's gifts, power and success. It is the same as jealousy. Now that he was in jail, they hoped to gain the honour and applause of the church.

2. Some preached in *strife and contention*. The strife was not over the gospel of substitution, but over words, practices, government, prophecy and less understood doctrines.

3. Some preached out of *a party spirit*. They were not sincere, but hoped to make Paul's chains more bitter. Paul met with trouble, punishment and prison; but they were preaching with little difficulty and opposition. Perhaps they thought that Paul's troubles were of his own making and that if he did things their way, he wouldn't have so much trouble!

4. Some preached Christ out of *love for Christ, for his church, for the lost and for Paul.* They knew that the apostle was in prison by the hand and providence of God, who does not act in the same way toward all his servants.

vv.18-20. What does it matter? Christ is preached in the glory of his person, in the fulness of his grace, in the excellency of his righteousness, in the efficacy of his sacrifice, in the power of his intercession. **'Therefore, I rejoice; and I will continue to rejoice.'**

'I know that all shall finally work together for my good (Rom. 8:28), even to my deliverance from prison to preach to you again' (in the same way as Peter was delivered from prison through the prayers of the church).

'This is my expectation and my desire — to magnify and glorify Christ, whether in prison or out, in life or in death. I am not ashamed of the gospel. I am not ashamed of the chains which hold me. I am not ashamed to die in prison.'

vv.21,22. **'For to me to live is Christ.'** He is the giver of life.

He is the sum and substance of life. He is the hope of life eternal — to be with him and to be like him. '**And to die is gain.**' I will gain release from pain and receive a perfect body, release from limited knowledge to a perfect mind, release from a sinful nature to a sinless perfection, release from all trials to perfect glory and joy, release from mortality to immortality!

'If it is the will of Christ for me to live longer in the flesh, I will continue to labour in the Lord's vineyard. I trust to have a fruitful labour. I can say nothing as to my own preference, for it is not mine to choose; the decision is the Lord's.'

vv.23,24. 'I must be honest, however. I am hard-pressed between these two thoughts: either to live and labour, or to die and be with Christ. To die and be with Christ would be better for me. But for me to remain here is better for you. It is best for me to go and be with Christ. It is best for you and the churches for me to remain and preach the gospel to you.'

vv.25,26. Paul had no divine revelation on this matter as such, but as he considered all things and examined his own heart, he felt confidently that God would deliver him and send him forth to preach again.

vv.27-30. The following verses are instructions.

1. 'Conduct your churches, homes and personal lives in a way that is becoming to the gospel you profess. Live, walk and talk as believers should.'

2. 'Whether I visit you or not, let me hear from others that you are standing together in unity and spirit, that you are contending together for the true gospel of Christ.'

3. 'Do not be afraid of your enemies. The fact that men oppose you for the sake of the gospel is evidence of their condemnation and of your salvation.'

4. 'It is not only ordained of God that you believe on Christ, but also that you suffer for his glory and your good.'

5. 'We are all in the same battle, you and I.'

Christian unity and humility

Philippians 2:1-14

This chapter is an exhortation to unity of spirit, mutual affection and love for one another, humility and lowliness of mind and real concern and care for one another.

vv.1,2. Our Master said, 'If you love me, keep my commandments.' John said, 'If they had been of us, they no doubt would have continued with us.' Paul uses the same argument in these verses.

1. **'If there be any comfort and confidence in Christ,'** that is, if you have a genuine reason for hope in Christ founded on his person, his righteousness and his death and intercession.

2. **'If there be any comfort and strength in love,'** the love of the Father for us which is everlasting; the love of the Son who gave himself for us; the love of the Holy Spirit, our Comforter, and the love of brethren, which is so pleasant and delightful.

3. **'If there be any fellowship of the Spirit,'** — if there is such a thing as a union of spirits, a oneness of heart and communion with one another.

4. **'If there is any bowels and mercy'** — if there is any real depth to your affection, and real compassion and concern for one another, then **fulfil ye my joy**. I rejoice in the evidence of your being complete and entire by living together in unity, love, mutual concern and respect, and by having the same purpose. Be of one mind in the gospel of grace, the glory of Christ and the work of the church. This reveals the grace of God in you' (James 2:26).

v.3. When things are done through strife, it involves quarrelling, contention and dividing into bitter camps. It leads to division. This is not the Spirit of Christ. We are not to do things seeking recognition and personal praise; this is empty

vainglory. In humility and sincerity, let us regard the other
brother as spiritually superior to ourselves. Paul said, 'I am less
than the least of the saints.' Be ready to give way to the judgement and desires of others as they are in accord with the
Scriptures.

v.4. **'Look not every man on his own interests but on the
interests and welfare of others.'** Paul is still talking mainly of
church fellowship. A man must have concern for his relationship with Christ, the right ordering of his home and children,
his business and his other responsibilities; he is not to leave
these to the care of others! He ought to be as concerned for
the welfare of his brother in Christ as he is for his own comforts. Respecting spiritual things and spiritual gifts, a believer
should not seek to have his own way, but should consult the
glory of Christ, the will of the Spirit and the general good and
peace of all the church.

vv.5-11. Having called for unity of spirit and purpose, love
and humility among brethren and sincere compassion and
concern for one another, Paul uses the example of our Lord
Jesus Christ.
   v.5. 'Let that humility be seen in you that was in Christ.'
Let this same attitude be in you that was in Christ. Let Christ
be your example of humility and lowliness of mind.
   v.6. Although being essentially one with God, Christ did
not seek to obtain it by force and robbery, as did Satan and
Adam. He was God and was with God in the beginning. He did
not in any showy display exhibit his glory and power.
   v.7. Rather, he stripped himself of all privileges and right-
ful dignity and became a mere man, a carpenter and a friend of
sinners.
   v.8. He was really a man, not just in appearance, but in
reality. He lay nine months in a womb; he lay in a manger; he
knew hunger, thirst, weariness, grief, pain and death. His real
submission and obedience, from the cradle to the cross, is our
example — not only our righteousness (Rom. 5:19), but our
example!
   vv.9-11. God, the Father, has highly exalted and rewarded
him.

v.12. 'Wherefore (staying with our subject and example), since you have heard my teachings and have obeyed the exhortations of God (whether I preached them to you in person or by letter, **work out** these Christian attitudes and principles,' which are called '**your salvation**' (not of your souls, but the deliverance of the church from strife and division). Do it in fear and trembling, not in fear of men or fear of damnation, but with serious caution and humility, lest we disturb and destroy the fellowship of the church which our Lord purchased with his own blood.

v.13. 'This attitude of humility and this spirit of love and unity are not of your own doing; but it is God who energizes and creates in you the desire and the ability to do his good pleasure. Your unity is his pleasure.'

v.14. 'Do all things without murmuring, grumbling, or finding fault, either with God or the brethren.
   Let brethren all agree, and peace among them spread;
   Old and young, rich and poor, are one in Christ, their Head.
   Among the saints on earth, let fervent love be found,
   Sons of our great God, with common blessings crowned;
   Let pride, that child of hell, be banished far away;
   Those should in humility dwell, who the same Lord obey.

The importance of faithful ministers

Philippians 2:14-30

vv.14,15. In the preceding verses Paul exhorts to us Christian unity, sincere love, humility and care, and concern for the needs and welfare of others. All good things which accompany salvation (whether civil, moral, or spiritual), no matter how disagreeable to our flesh, are to be done without murmuring against the will of God or disputing among ourselves.

'**That ye may be blameless and harmless, the sons of God,**' in the sight of men, not in the sight of God. In Christ we are blameless before God. In Christ we are sons of God. Paul is saying that our attitude, conversation and conduct before our brethren and the wicked of this world should be such that they cannot charge us with hypocrisy and insincerity. We are to be lights and examples to those about us, 'that they may see our good works and glorify our Father' (Matt. 5:16). In short, let us speak and live as sons of God ought (Rom. 12:1,2).

v.16.   '**Holding out** and offering to men **the word of life**,' the gospel of our Lord Jesus (1 Tim. 4:16; Titus 2:10). If these two things are present in and among you, then I have not laboured in vain and I will be able to rejoice with you in the day of glory. Your conduct and character reveal that you are one with Christ (sons of God) and that you are burdened and concerned that others come to know the Lord Jesus. Love for Christ and love for others will constrain us to please him and to evangelize them! (Matt. 22:36-40; Gal. 5:14).

vv.17,18.   Paul had been the means God used to bring the Philippian believers to Christ. He also believed that he would be killed for preaching the gospel; thus he says, 'Do not be sorrowful when you hear of my death and the pouring out of my blood for the sake of the gospel; but rejoice with me, for I am ready not only to be bound but to die for Christ's sake' (Acts 21:13; 5:41).

v.19.   Paul wished to send Timothy to visit the church (and preach to them) that he might know of their general spiritual welfare, how the gospel stood with them, how they kept the ordinances, how their ministers preached, etc. Notice how Paul proposes this: '**I trust in the Lord Jesus to send Timothy.**' Even the apostle Paul subjected his intentions, desires and plans to the will of our Lord! (Rom. 8:26: James 4:13-15).

vv.20,21.   This is a serious charge, but unfortunately true. Not all ministers are genuinely interested in the glory of Christ and the good of their congregations. Rather, they seek to advance their own interests. Timothy had a heart and soul like Paul's! He preached the gospel of God's glory and grace. He sought not his own comfort and praise, but he cared for the spiritual welfare of the people (Ezek. 34:1-6).

vv.22-24. 'You know Timothy's value and worth. He was with me when I preached to you at the first. He was as a son to me in the labours of the Lord. I trust that I shall also be able to visit you.' Our Lord uses his ministers to teach, set in order and lead his church. We are not to despise our true spiritual leaders, but to respect and follow them as they follow Christ (Eph. 4:10-16; Phil. 2:29).

vv.25-30. Meanwhile, before Paul or Timothy could come to preach and minister to them, Epaphroditus, one of their own ministers, would return to them. He had been sent to Rome with presents from them to Paul. While at Rome (or on the journey to Rome), he became ill and was at the point of death. Believers have natural bodies and are subject to illness the same as all men, but God had compassion on him and healed him (James 5:15,16).

No confidence in the flesh

Philippians 3:1-11

v.1. Paul begins chapter 3 with the theme and watchword of every believer: **'Rejoice in our Lord.'** Christ Jesus is our chief joy:

1. In the greatness of his person, very God of very God;
2. In the fitness of his incarnation, bone of our bone and flesh of our flesh;
3. In the sufficiency of his righteousness and atonement;
4. In the comforts of his providence and purpose;
5. In the glory of his intercession and return.

'To write the same things to you is not tiresome.' He rejoices to repeat the gospel of Christ over and over, for it is necessary.

1. It keeps your thoughts and hearts on Christ, the Foundation.

2. It keeps you from the errors of false teachers.

3. When truth is repeated, it guards you against self-righteousness and other errors.

v.2.   These are the false teachers from the Jews, who were imposing the works and ceremonies of the law upon the Gentiles as being necessary to salvation. Paul uses the same name on them which they used to give to the Gentiles — **'dogs!'** He calls them **'evil workers'** because they misled the people, deceived them and perverted the gospel of Christ. **'Beware of the circumcisers'** (those who mutilate the flesh for sanctifying purposes). Circumcision served its day as a token of the covenant and may be recommended as a hygienic measure, but it has no place or meaning in the covenant of grace.

v.3.   'We are the true circumcision, not they. They have the name, the form, the outward sign. We have in Christ and in the new birth its fulfilment'. It is the difference between having the lamb of the Old Testament sacrifice and having Christ, the Lamb of God.

1. True circumcision is having the heart pricked and laid open by the Spirit.

2. True circumcision is a renouncing of our own righteousness.

3. True circumcision is of the heart, not the flesh.

4. It is to draw nigh to God with the heart, not the body.

5. It is to rejoice in our completeness in Christ, having no confidence in carnal descent, tribe or family, ceremony or law. Our salvation and acceptance by God are only in Christ, not in anything connected with this flesh. We worship God in heart and in Spirit, not in outward rituals and ceremonies. We rejoice in Christ, in whom we are complete (Col. 2:9,10). We have no confidence in our own fleshly works nor in anyone else.

v.4.   Paul illustrates the point using himself: 'If there is any value in our family ties, ceremonies, religious works and performances, outward obedience to law and rites, I have more room to boast than any of these false teachers.'

vv.5,6. Paul was circumcised the eighth day, of the stock of Israel (not an Ishmaelite or a proselyte, but a natural Israelite), of the tribe of Benjamin (this tribe was from Jacob and Rachel and kept true worship when ten revolted), had a Hebrew mother and a Hebrew father, was a Pharisee (the strictest sect of the Jews, held in highest esteem), persecuted the church, and with respect to the observance of the outward law, was blameless.

v.7. At one time he felt that all these things were necessary for acceptance with God, were necessary for righteousness and entitled him to the favour of God. When God revealed Christ to him, he saw all these things to be worthless in themselves. Christ is our sacrifice, our sanctification and our righteousness. He is the fulfilment of all these. That which was everything to Paul became nothing; Christ became everything (Col. 3:11).

v.8. 'Furthermore, I count everything as loss compared to that priceless privilege (that overwhelming advantage) of knowing Christ Jesus, my Lord. For his sake I lost everything in order that I may have Christ, the Redeemer.'

    1. He renounced not only the Jewish ceremonies, but worldly honour, reputation, substance, comforts and advantages.

    2. He lost self-righteousness and gained Christ's righteousness.

    3. He lost ceremonial bondage and gained his freedom.

    4. He lost false peace and gained true peace with God.

    5. He lost pretended glory and gained eternal glory (1 Cor. 1:30,31).

vv.9-11. This is my determined purpose, my one desire, my soul and heart's sincere hope, which is threefold:

    1. **'That I may win Christ and be found in him,'** not trusting or having any self-achieved righteousness in works and deeds,

possessing that genuine righteousness of God which comes through faith in Christ — that holiness and perfect righteousness which he gives to his own (Col. 1:22).

2. **'That I may really know him.'** I do know him, but I want progressively to become more deeply and intimately acquainted with him and the wonders of his person; that I may come to know the power flowing from his resurrection and the strength it gives to believers; that I may so know and share his sufferings as to be transformed continually into his likeness, daily dying to sin and the world.

3. **'That I might attain unto the resurrection of the dead.'** Paul may be referring here to the resurrection of the body in the likeness of Christ in the great day of our Lord. However (because of the next verse), I believe he is talking about a moral and spiritual resurrection that lifts us out of the death and darkness of the world and sin. The world, the flesh and all of this human life are death. In Christ there is real life, real love, real holiness. There is communion with God and perfect righteousness. This is what I want. By whatever means it pleases God to bring me to this place, I want to be like Christ in attitude, spirit and heart.

Forgetting the past - holding the present - anticipating the future

Philippians 3:12-21

v.12. I have not attained to perfect holiness, perfect knowledge, nor perfect happiness. Though my sanctification is perfect in Christ, it is not perfected in me. I know in part, sin dwells in me, my faith is imperfect, but I press on. I long to lay hold on that for which Christ laid hold of me. I want what the Lord purposed and purchased for me on Calvary — to be like him! (Eph. 1:3-6.)

v.13. 'Brethren, I don't claim to have arrived at perfection in doctrine, spirit, nor deed. I am not yet all that Christ would have me to be. I am not all that I would like to be, nor even all that I ought to be. Thank God, however, I am not what I used to be! **One thing I do**: I forget what lies behind me — my struggles and attempts at self-righteousness in false religion, my experiences and revelations in spiritual infancy, my works and labours since conversion, my recent growth and revelations. Now I reach forth for present and future blessings and revelations of his grace.' The illustration is taken from runners in a race, who do not stop to look behind them to see how far they have come nor to determine how far they are in front of others, but they are concerned for what they are doing now and for what lies ahead.

v.14. 'My goal and aim is to finish the race and obtain the supreme and heavenly prize — the incorruptible crown of life, righteousness and glory!' (Ps. 17:15.) We look to Christ (Heb. 12:1,2). We follow and depend on Christ (1 John 3:1-3).

v.15. 'Let all of us who are spiritually mature (who are taught of God) have this same mind and hold these same convictions:

1. To count all heritage, ceremony, tradition and works of religion as rubbish that we may win Christ and be found in him.

2. To be willing to suffer the loss of all things for a knowledge of Christ.

3. To disclaim perfection in ourselves, but to aim for it.

4. To desire to be found in him, having his righteousness.

5. To desire above all things to be like Christ and press forward in perseverance to attain that incorruptible crown.'

v.16. Nevertheless, whatever degree of the knowledge of Christ and the truth of the gospel and the light we have received, let us walk therein! As we walk in the light that God gives us, he will give more light.

Here I raise my Ebenezer;
Hither by thy help I'm come.

My spiritual growth may be slow, even discouraging. Sometimes I may feel that I am standing still. But I know that God has revealed Christ in me, and I know whom I have believed. I will hold fast to this until he reveals more of himself.

v. 17.   'Follow me,' Paul says, 'as I follow Christ.' Paul would not have any man follow him as the head of a party or sect. He condemned others for that. He wanted them to have the same goal he had — to win Christ and be found in him! 'Also, observe others who live after this pattern I have set for you.' Believers should encourage and be examples to one another in the pursuit of righteousness (Matt. 5:16; Titus 2:10).

vv. 18, 19.   'I have told you often and now tell you with great sorrow that many religious people walk a road which reveals them as enemies of the cross. They hold to ceremony and circumcision, not Christ alone. They glory in the flesh, making merchandise of you. They are more interested in converts than in conversions, more interested in statistics than in spirituality, more interested in gifts than in the Giver. They turn the grace of God into a licence to sin. Their end is destruction. Their god is not the living God, but their own desires and passions. What they glory in is really what they ought to be ashamed of; they are concerned for carnal, earthly, fleshly things.' Someone said, 'God created us to love people and use things, but sinful men love things and use people.'

vv. 20, 21.   Our citizenship and interests are in heaven, not tied to this world. In Christ we are sons of God, seated in him, heirs of eternal glory and we patiently wait for his return. All we are, have and hope to be is in Christ. He will complete the work he has begun by changing our vile bodies into the glory and majesty of his own body, exerting the power which enables him to subject everything to himself (1 Cor. 15:51-55).

Think on these things

Philippians 4:1-8

v.1. 'My brethren,' not in the natural sense but in a spiritual sense, having the same Father, being in the same family, of the household of faith.

'My dearly beloved and longed for.' Paul sincerely loved these people and longed to be with them, to fellowship and converse with them.

'My joy and my crown.' He taught them the gospel and they were seals of his ministry and proof of his call. They were a greater joy and crown to him than anything that the world could offer. The fruits of a man's ministry are his converts and they are the best test of his ministry (Matt. 7:15-20).

'Stand fast in the Lord.'

1. Stand fast in his power, for even saints are liable to fall (Jude 24).

2. Stand fast in his gospel, which is able to save (1 Cor. 15:1).

3. Stand fast in the liberty of Christ, as opposed to the bondage of the law.

4. Stand fast in the doctrines of Christ (1 Tim. 4:16).

v.2. Two women, Euodias and Syntyche (members of the church), evidently were divided over a problem. Paul takes notice of their conflict and exhorts them to settle it for the glory of God and to be united in fellowship and purpose. All believers should seek to preserve the unity of the church and to be of the same mind (Col. 3:12-15).

v.3. This is evidently addressed to the pastor, who was to assist these women in settling their differences. These women were of valuable aid to Paul, Clement and others. Let us help bring people together, for the unity of the church and the glory of Christ are much more important than personal differences and disputes.

v.4. The word 'rejoice' is used ten times in this epistle. I pray that we may learn the word in heart and experience as well as in doctrine. There is always cause to rejoice in the Lord! Rejoice in his grace, which is always sufficient. Rejoice in his blood, which cleanses. Rejoice in his righteousness, which justifies. Rejoice in his love, which never fails. Rejoice in his providence, which works all things together for our good. Rejoice in his intercession, which is continual. Rejoice that your names are written in the book of life!

v.5. The 'moderation' here is not in eating and drinking, though this is certainly important. The word here is 'Let all men (both in the church and out) see and recognize your humility, unselfishness, consideration and forgiving spirit.'

1. We are to deal with others not with the severity of law and justice, but with gentleness and love (Eph. 4:31,32).

2. We are to put up with affronts and injuries by bearing them patiently and forgivingly.

3. We are to put the best interpretation on words and statements, not seeking cause for offence.

4. Let our Christian attitude adorn our doctrine, for '**the Lord is at hand,**' meaning 'he will help you by giving you grace,' or 'the Lord observes our conduct of spirit,' or 'the Lord is coming soon to judge all men.' All are true.

v.6. 'Do not fret, murmur, nor be filled with anxiety over things (Ps. 37:1-8). Take your burdens, cares and problems to the Lord in prayer. In everything let your requests be known to God, and do it with thanksgiving.' I can never come to the throne for mercy except I already have mercies for which to be thankful!

v.7. This '**peace of God**' is twofold.

1. It is the peace which is made with God by the obedience, sacrifice and intercession of our blessed Lord (Rom. 5:1).

2. It is the peace of heart, mind and conscience which arises

from a correct view of Christ. We know that we have passed from death to life; we know that our sins are forgiven; we know that we are sons of God and the peace of God rules in our hearts.

'**Passeth understanding.**' The natural man certainly does not understand this peace and rest which Christ gives. His soul and mind are in a constant state of unrest and turmoil. Neither do we fully understand the blessed peace of God which he in mercy gives us in Christ! We accept it by faith and rest in his promise.

v.8. '**Finally, brethren.**' In this matter of attitude and humble spirit, '**think on these things!**' Meditate on them. Consider and dwell upon them in order to put them into daily practice:

1. '**Whatsoever things are true**' — agreeable to the truth in Christ Jesus, the truth of the gospel and the Word of God.

2. '**Whatsoever things are honest**' — honest in the sight of God and men, honest in business, in speech, in conduct.

3. '**Whatsoever things are just**' — giving to God that which is his (worship, praise, reverence, myself) and to man that which is his, avoiding oppression and injustice. Owe no man anything he needs or deserves.

4. '**Whatsoever things are pure**' — pure in word or deed, in opposition to pride, covetousness, hatred, envy and self-seeking.

5. '**Whatsoever things are holy**' — agreeable to the character of God and his kingdom, that which promotes holiness of heart and life.

6. '**Whatsoever things are lovely.**' These are faith, kindness, compassion, generosity and all commendable virtues.

7. '**Whatsoever things are of good report**' — things which contribute to a good name, a good reputation, a good opinion for the glory of Christ.

If anything is virtuous and worthy of praise, think on these things. 'As a man thinketh in his heart, so is he!' (Prov. 4:23).

The support of missionaries and preachers

Philippians 4:9-23

v.9.   Throughout this epistle Paul has exhorted the people to have unity of spirit and purpose, to love one another, to have real concern and care for one another, to be of a humble mind and disposition, to avoid false teachers, to rest in Christ alone for righteousness and to meditate on holy things. Now in this verse he makes a very important point: '**Those things which you have learned and received.**' It is hoped that you have not just learned these things in a doctrinal way, but that you have received them not just in your head, but in your heart! And you have not only 'heard them from me, but you have **seen them in me**'. What good are words if our actions and attitudes are contrary? '**Do** these things! Put them in daily practice. **God will be with you!**'

v.10.   Paul rejoiced over the gifts and supplies this church had sent him by their pastor. Evidently they had for some reason neglected to communicate with him for a long time. He adds, 'I'm sure you were thinking of me, but you had no opportunity to show it.' Let this be a lesson to us: let us always be faithful in our prayers, care and concern for those who labour faithfully in the Word. Don't forget those missionaries and ministers whom you do not see for a season.

v.11.   Paul did not mean to imply that he was wanting anything, though he possessed nothing. He had all things in Christ and found contentment and peace in whatever condition the providence of God put him, be it adversity or prosperity, with much or little (Luke 12:15; 1 Tim. 6:6-10). He learned this in the school of grace, taught by the Spirit.

v.12.   'I know how to be treated with contempt by men, to

live humbly in a low condition, to work with my hands, to be
hungry and cold — yet not to be depressed, cast down or
murmur against God. I know how to be held in the esteem of
men, to have an abundance — yet not to be lifted up with
pride and forget that "the Lord giveth and the Lord taketh
away". I have learned of God how to behave toward the
temporary things of earth, how to put them in their proper
perspective.'

v. 13.   And now, lest he be thought to be proud of his grace
and ascribe too much to himself, he attributes all grace to the
power of Christ in him. 'I can be happy in any state and
endure all these things, not in my own strength (for no man
was more conscious of his own weakness than Paul). I am
ready for anything through the power of Christ in me.'

> Content with beholding his face, my all to his pleasure
> resigned;
> No changes of season or place would make any change in
> my mind.
> While blest with a sense of his love, a palace a toy would
> appear;
> And prisons would palaces prove if Jesus would dwell with
> me there.

v. 14.   Paul adds this lest they should think that he was
discounting their gift and was not grateful. He has declared, 'I
can be content in need or in plenty, but I appreciate your help.
You have done what you should have done. You have done
well in providing for those who preach God's Word' (1 Cor.
9:6-11).

vv. 15-17.   This church was the only church that talked with
Paul about the subject of giving and supporting the ministry of
the Word. Even when he left Philippi and went to Thessalonica,
they supported his ministry and took care of his needs. Strange
that, even in the days of the apostles, churches were negligent
in the matter of missions and supporting missionaries. He says,
'I have not entered into this subject because I desire a gift
from you. I am eager to see the fruits of righteousness and

salvation in you. The kingdom of God can get along without you and me, but I would like to see some evidence that you and I are in that kingdom of grace' (James 2:14-20).

vv.18,19.   'I have in hand all of your gifts, sent to me through your pastor. These gifts have the sweet smell of an offering and sacrifice which God welcomes and in which he delights. I cannot repay you, but my God will! He shall supply all your needs according to his riches in glory through Christ Jesus!'

v.20.   To God, who is our Father in Christ Jesus, be all the glory for the grace he gives now, for the glory and happiness expected and for the supply of every need, both temporal and spiritual.

vv.21-23.   'Greet all the brethren there. The brethren and believers here send their greetings to you. The grace of our Lord Jesus be with you!'

Colossians

The Colossian letter

Colossians 1:1-8

Date uncerta   *55 AD ?*

This letter to the church at Colosse was written about thirty years after Christ died on the cross. Paul wrote it while in prison at Rome, about the same time that he wrote Philippians and Ephesians.

Who brought the gospel to Colosse and when, we do not know. Paul had never preached to them (2:1). The city was destroyed six years later by an earthquake and later rebuilt.

The occasion for the letter was that Epaphras, who had preached to them, came to Rome and told Paul about their faith and love. He also reported their danger from false teachers who had come among them — Judaizers, who urged the ceremonies of the law, and Gentiles, who promoted philosophy, worship of angels and saints, will-worship and punishing the body. Paul wrote to them to confirm them in the gospel of Christ, to warn them of spiritual error and to exhort them to a discharge of their duty to God, to one another and to all men.

v.1. **'Paul, an apostle of Jesus Christ, by the will of God.'** In the beginning of the Christian church there were apostles.

1. They were chosen by Christ.
2. They saw the Lord personally.
3. They had infallible knowledge of the gospel, inspired by the Holy Spirit.
4. They were gifted to work miracles for the confirmation of their doctrine.

All of this was by the will of God, as the Father's will and the Son's work are the same. There are no apostles in the church today!

'And Timothy, our brother.' While Timothy was not an apostle, Paul included him in the salutation, for the highest

office-bearer in the church recognizes even the least as being a
brother and worthy of respect and recognition. In Christ we
are one, and he that is greatest is but a servant.

v.2.   **'To the saints and faithful brethren in Christ.'** All
believers are saints and all believers are faithful brethren. We
are sanctified by the Father, the Son and the Spirit. We are
brethren because firstly, we have the same Father, secondly,
we are in one body and family and, thirdly, we have all one
elder Brother, Christ Jesus. The key word is 'in Christ'! We are
saints and brethren because we are in Christ.

   'Grace be unto you and peace.' Moses prayed, 'Lord, if I
have found grace in thy sight, show me thy way' (Exod. 33:13).
Where God's grace is given, all other things will follow —
peace, joy, rest and more. 'Grace' first; then 'peace'.

vv.3-5.   This is Paul's prayer of thanksgiving for these faithful
brethren.

   1. **'We give thanks to God.'** All things are of God: that is,
our salvation, faith, hope, love (Ps. 103:1-5). 'I am what I am
by the grace of God' (1 Cor. 15:10). Every spiritual gift is
from God through our Lord Jesus Christ (John 3:27; James
1:17).

   2. He thanked God for their **'faith'** in the first place.
Without faith there can be no union with Christ (Mark 16:16);
there can be no benefit from Christ (Heb. 11:6).

   3. He thanked God for their **'love'** for one another (1 Cor.
13:13). Love is the evidence of faith (John 13:35). Love is the
fruit of faith (Gal. 5:22). The absence of love reveals the
absence of God (1 John 4:8).

   4. He thanked God for their **'hope'**. The believer's inheritance is not in his hand yet. He has it in hope! Our hope is as
certain as the purpose of the Father, the atonement of the Son
and the witness of the Spirit. It is still hope, however, until it
becomes a reality. We really have little to expect or hope for
on this earth, but all things are ours in Christ — this is our
hope! We heard of it in the gospel. It is the gospel that is God's
instrument to beget faith and hope in the heart (Rom. 10:17;
1 Peter 1:3).

v.6.   Having mentioned the gospel which begets faith, hope and love, he says,

1. '**It came to you**. You didn't come to it. God sent it to you.' He is 'found of those who sought him not' (Rom. 10:20; Gal. 1:15; 1 John 4:10).

2. The gospel '**bringeth forth fruit**' (Isa. 55:11). It brings forth the fruit of faith, love, joy, peace; we are new creatures in Christ. A seed that does not produce fruit is not the seed of the Word.

3. The gospel continues to produce fruit. '**Since the day you heard the gospel and knew the grace of God it has brought forth fruit.**'

vv.7,8.   Having confirmed the gospel, he commends the preacher.

1. He is commended for being a '**fellow servant**' of Christ with Paul.

2. He is praised for being a '**faithful minister** of Christ'.

3. He is commended for his respect for them, for he declared their love and faith in Christ. It is a good sign when one speaks well of those who are absent.

Made fit for heaven

Colossians 1:9-17

vv.9-11.   '**For this cause we also, since the day we heard of it, do not cease to pray for you.**' Their pastor, Epaphras, had declared unto Paul the love the Colossians had for Christ and for one another. This brought forth from Paul a prayer of thanksgiving and a prayer for their further growth in grace, wisdom and understanding. The believers' graces at their best are imperfect and subject to decay (1 Cor. 13:9; Rev. 2:4) and may be abused (2 Cor. 12:7). Therefore Paul prays for them.

1. '**That you may be filled with the knowledge of his will.**' This is the revealed will of God, to be learned from his Word

and in his Son: his will of redemption, his will of purpose, his will of conduct and attitude and his will of eternal glory. He prayed not only that they should have a knowledge of these, but be 'filled' inwardly with a knowledge of his 'wisdom and spiritual understanding'. Oh, that we may be delivered from the dead letter of the law and the dry tradition of religious orthodoxy! That we may have wisdom and spiritual under-standing of our sins, our need and our inability! That we may have understanding of God's manifold mercies in Christ — how he can be just and Justifier, of the riches of his grace in his kindness toward us in Christ! May ours be not a profession of religion but a true possession of Christ.

2. 'That ye might walk worthy of the Lord unto all pleasing.' This is our godly conduct and behaviour, not only in the church, but in the home, on the job and on the street. We will live and talk as those who are in Christ, seeking to please and glorify God.

'Being fruitful in every good work.' Believers are trees of righteousness, planted by the Lord to bear the fruit of the Spirit and good works of the kingdom of Christ (Eph. 2:10).

'Increasing in the knowledge of God.' Ignorance in believers dishonours God as much as fruitlessness! Both fruitfulness and a growth in knowledge of our Lord are necessary to walk worthy of the Lord!

3. 'Strengthened with all might according to his glorious power.' We are not expected to walk worthy of the Lord, be fruitful and grow in grace and knowledge in our own strength and power, but in his! (2 Cor. 12:9.) This power and grace will enable us to bear afflictions and trials with patience, persever-ance and real joy. His power and grace will subdue the whole man — his hand, his heart and his tongue! (Ps. 37:1-8.)

v.12.   Paul is continually giving thanks to God. Here he gives thanks that God (by his grace in Christ) has qualified us, has made us fit, to partake of heaven, the bright and glorious inheritance of the saints. Every man in his natural state is unfit for heaven and God's presence! However, he has given us in Christ all that we need! (1 Cor. 1:30.)

vv.13,14.   He explains how God makes us qualified and fit
for heaven by drawing us out of that corrupt state in which we
were born and translating us into the state of grace, called **'the
kingdom of his dear Son'** (Rom. 14:17). This he does in
effectual regeneration by his Spirit. He redeems us from sin,
the law, his justice and wrath by the blood of his Son. No way
of redemption can be accepted that does not totally ransom
the sinner, fully honour God's law and completely satisfy his
justice.

v.15.   The apostle, having spoken of our redemption, takes
up a description of the redeemer!
   'He is the image of the invisible God.' Christ is the exact
likeness of the unseen God. He is the visible representation in
the flesh of the invisible God (John 14:8-10; 2 Cor. 5:19).
Every attribute of God is seen in Christ (Heb. 1:1-3).
   'The first-born of every creature.' This does not mean that
he was the first of creation, or the first creature made, for in
the next verse it is said that all things were created by him. But
Paul is saying he is the King, Lord and Owner of all creation.
The Jews make the first-born to be synonymous with 'king'.
He is the King, Owner and Heir of all creation, for it was all
made by him.

vv.16,17.   It was by him and in him that all things were
created and by him that all things are held together.

Christ - The Head of the church

Colossians 1:18-29

v.18.   **'Christ is the head of the body, the church.'** By the
church is meant the whole election of grace, every believer of
all generations (Eph. 5:23-27). He is the representative Head
from all eternity and in all time. He is the political Head, in
that he reigns. He is the economical Head, in that he provides

every need (1 Cor. 1:30). Without a vital union with Christ we would be as dead as a body without a head!

'Christ is the beginning.' He is the root, or foundation cause, of the church. We were chosen in him; from him all spiritual life flows. As Eve was from Adam, so the church is from Christ. It is a body of his preparing.

'Christ is the first-born from the dead.' He was the first who rose from the dead by his own power to immortality and life. He is the pledge of resurrection for us. 'Because I live, ye shall live also' (John 14:19). Death has no more power or claim on him.

'That in all things he might have the pre-eminence.' That he might have first place in our affection, in our thoughts, in our desires to be like him and in the highest praise of our lips. He is the first:

1. In sonship; no one is a son in the sense he is.
2. In election; he is the first chosen and we are chosen in him.
3. In covenant; he is the Surety, Mediator and Messenger.
4. In redemption; he wrought it and bought it.
5. In life; he quickeneth whom he will.
6. In death and resurrection; he conquered death, hell and the grave. He ought to have pre-eminence.

vv.19,20.   It is true that all the fulness of the Godhead dwells in Christ (Col. 2:9). He is God (2 Cor. 5:19). God dwells in the body of Christ as he dwelt in the tabernacle. This fulness, however, is the fulness of complete redemption which he is able to give to believers:

1. The fulness of wisdom, holiness and righteousness.
2. The fulness of grace, peace and joy.
3. The fulness of eternal life and glory.

'We are complete in him' (Col. 2.10).

All of the elect, whether already in heaven or on the earth, are by his blood reconciled and brought to peace with God (Rom. 5:1-10).

vv.21,22.   What Paul had said about reconciliation in general in the preceding verse, he applies to the Colossians in particular.

We need to embrace these verses personally. We were strangers, enemies in our minds (Rom. 8:7), workers of iniquity. However, in the body of his flesh, by his perfect obedience and the merits of his blood, he has so reconciled us to God that we are and will be presented before God in that day free from all sin, perfect in holiness and without one charge against us (Rom. 8:33,34; Jude 24). He has reconciled! It is finished! The work is done!

v.23. 'If you continue in the faith and be not moved away from the hope of the gospel.' All of the preceding provisions and promises are ours only if we persevere or continue in faith. Nothing but judgement awaits those who depart from Christ (Heb. 10:38,39; 3:6,14; 2 Tim. 4:6-8). God keeps us through, and not apart from, faith (1 Peter 1:5; Jer. 32:40).

vv.24,25. Twice in verses 23-25 Paul says, 'I am made a minister.' All believers are witnesses and preachers of the gospel, but there are certain offices and responsibilities in the body of Christ to which men are specifically called and equipped. Paul was an apostle, sent to preach the gospel, suffer certain afflictions and endure certain trials for the sake of the church. He rejoiced that he was entrusted with the gospel, counted worthy to suffer for Christ's sake and to preach fully the gospel of Christ.

v.26. This gospel of Christ (his incarnation, his nature and his person, office, death, resurrection and salvation) given to lost sinners is an ancient gospel, and it is not understood by the natural mind. It is called a mystery! (1 Cor. 2:7-14.) The gospel was before veiled in promises, sacrifices, ceremonies and prophecies; but is now made manifest (or revealed to believers) by the Holy Spirit. Without his revelation, it remains profound and mysterious. Those who have the clearest knowledge know only in part (1 Cor. 13:9; 8:1,2).

v.27. God, by his Spirit and his ministers, would make known to you the riches of the glory of this gospel. He has laid out the great and unsearchable treasures of his mercy, his grace,

his goodness, his righteousness. He has revealed all of the glory
of his wisdom, mercy, justice and truth. All of this dwells in
Christ! It is ours in Christ. We possess the riches of his grace
and we hope for eternal glory as Christ dwells in us by faith
(Col. 2:3).

v.28.   Paul had a twofold message: **'warning every man'** and
'instructing every man'. Someone said, 'The blessings of God
are hedged about on one side by the warnings of God, lest any
presume, and on the other side by the promises of God, lest
any despair.' It is the duty of the minister to warn the careless
of God's wrath to come and to invite men to flee to Christ.

v.29.   'Therefore I labour,' according to the grace and strength
he gives!

Complete in him - 1

Colossians 2:1-7

vv. 1-5.   The apostle wanted the people of Colosse to know
what great concern he had for them (and for believers every-
where), even though he had never met them personally. He
then gave reasons for this conflict and concern.
1.   *v.2.*   **'That your hearts might beat as one in love for
Christ and one another.'** This is the way to comfort. Lack of
unity of heart and affection will destroy joy and comfort.
2.   *v.2.*   'That your hearts may beat as one in **understanding** and **acknowledging** the gospel of the glory of the Father
and the Son (which is called in the preceding chapter 'the
mystery of God'). Union of heart in affection depends much
upon common understanding and belief of the main truths
concerning Christ and how God saves sinners. 'Two will not
long walk together in spiritual love who do not agree on
spiritual truth.' Let us pray for a growth in the knowledge of
Christ and his grace.

3. *v.3.* In Christ are stored up all the riches of God's grace and glory. In him are stored all wisdom and knowledge. Don't look for anything pertaining to God's mercy, grace and righteousness anywhere but in Christ. There is in Christ everything necessary to salvation (1 John 5:20).

4. *v.4.* 'I say this with deep concern, lest any should mislead or deceive you, lest any should draw you away from the simplicity of Christ with beguiling speech' (2 Cor. 11:3). Satan endeavours to sow the seed of error wherever the gospel of Christ is preached. His chief weapon is to entice men to depart in any way from a full trust and confidence in Christ alone and to lean even partially on the flesh (Rom. 11:6).

5. *v.5.* **'I am absent from you in the flesh.'** If Paul had been there in person, he could have dealt with these errors as he dealt with Peter (Gal. 2:11-14). (We are to guard jealously the gospel of God's glory.) He was **'with them in spirit'**, however, rejoicing over their faith in Christ.

v.6. **'As ye have received Christ.'** How did you receive Christ? You received him:

1. As the sum and substance of all saving truth.

2. As the fulfilment of all promises.

3. As the fountain of all grace.

4. As the whole of acceptance and righteousness with and before God.

5. As the object of faith and love.

'In the same manner as you received him, continue to walk in him. Live day by day in this faith, trust and relationship. You don't begin in Christ and get perfected, comforted or accepted in your flesh' (Gal. 3:1-3).

v.7. In this verse Paul prescribes three means for attaining to a constant walk in Christ.

1. **'Rooted and built up in him.'** This is a metaphor taken from trees deeply rooted; 'rooted in him'. The grip with which faith lays hold on Christ is like a tree deeply rooted in the ground. Its strength, nourishment, life and fruit are supplied from him. Built up in him is a metaphor taken from a building fastened to a foundation. The shape and the stability of the

building are determined by the foundation (1 Cor. 3:11).

2. **'Established in the faith, as ye have been taught, and abounding therein,'** established in the doctrine of faith concerning Christ (Heb. 13:9). Not weary of old truths, not moved by new revelations from teachers who glory in the flesh, not easily offended, not driven about with every wind of doctrine, this 'building' is firmly established and growing in the faith of the Lord Jesus.

3. All of this is **'with thanksgiving'**. There is great reason for thanksgiving:

1. The unspeakable gift of Christ;
2. Faith itself, which is the gift of God;
3. The gospel and spiritual light;
4. True ministers;
5. All things in Christ (1 Thess. 5:18).

Complete in him - 2

Colossians 2:8-13

After expressing his great concern and care for the church at Colosse, Paul begins to warn them of false teachers and their errors.

v.8. In this verse the error of false religion is dealt with under three heads:

1. **'Philosophy.'** There is nothing wrong with true philosophy, but the Word of God is never to be subjected to human reason, and human philosophy is never to be introduced into the worship and service of God. 'Let God be true and every man a liar' (Rom. 3:4).

2. **'Tradition of men.'** These are practices and rites in the church without the authority of the written Word, having no warrant but custom and human tradition. For instance: infant baptism, mass, purgatory and prayers for the dead, the celebration of religious holidays such as Christmas, Easter and so forth.

3. **'Rudiments of the world.'** These are the Mosaical rites and ceremonies — circumcision, abstaining from certain meats, the observance of sabbath days and so forth. Since Christ has fulfilled all these, the practice of them is sinful. The way of Christ will not mix with man's philosophy, traditions, nor legal obedience!

v.9.   There is nothing that will make a believer look to Christ alone, cling to and rest in Christ alone, more than to realize that everything God is, that God requires and that the sinner needs is *in Christ* (1 Cor. 1:30). This is the third time that Paul has told the Colossians that all fulness is in Christ (see Col. 1:19; 2:3). You can add nothing to fulness!

v.10.   We are perfect in him! He is perfect, and our being in him makes us perfect. This is not speaking of what we shall be, but of what we are right now in Christ! Not in ourselves, but in him. He is the head of all principality and power (not only in the church, but angels, kings, rulers, religious heads, etc.) In him there is no charge, obligation, duty or service that can be demanded of us for redemption — not by anyone! (Col. 1:21,22.)

v.11.   Circumcision was instituted by God (Gen. 17:10-13).
    1. It was a token of the covenant, the promise of God's blessings.
    2. It was a sign by which Israel was distinguished from other nations.
    3. It is a picture of spiritual regeneration, circumcision of the heart, which is putting off the body and power of sin (Rom. 2:28,29).

    1. Circumcision was necessary to eating of Passover (Exod. 12:48).
    2. A child was named at circumcision (Luke 1:59; 2:21).
    3. Circumcision of heart brings us to the table of the Lord and gives us a new name — sons of God! All this we have in Christ. Thus, it is not necessary to circumcise the flesh.

v.12.   We are not only circumcised in Christ in a spiritual
sense (having the token, evidence and power of the covenant
of grace), but all our sins are buried with Christ (of which our
baptism in water is a representation)! Christ died for our sins
and was buried. When he arose, all our sins were left behind!
It is through faith that we see ourselves crucified, buried and
risen with Christ. It is not just any faith, but that which is of
God's operation!

v.13.   God raised Christ from the dead, and God must raise
us from the dead. We were dead in trespasses and sins (Eph.
2:1-8). Forgiveness of sin is not done piecemeal, but is done at
once and includes all sin — past, present and future (1 John
1:7).

When we savingly believe in Christ, we are at that moment
united to Christ. All that Christ did, suffered, or procured as
our Head (whether in his life, death, burial, resurrection, or
exaltation) is imputed to us by God, even to the right to all
these benefits, given to us as if we had been personally present
with him at those times and had done them all ourselves
(Eph. 1:3; 2:6).

Christ or ceremony

Colossians 2:14-23

In Christ we are complete (v.10). In Christ we have the seal of
the covenant upon our hearts (v.11). In Christ we are risen
from the dead (v.12). In Christ we are forgiven of all sins (v.13).

v.14.   When we think of handwriting, we think of the handwriting on the wall against Belshazzar: 'Thou art weighed in
the balances and found wanting.' This handwriting against us is
the whole ceremonial law of Moses, with its ordinances,
commandments and laws, plus the moral law. We are weighed
and found wanting (Rom. 3:19,23). None but Christ could

put away this handwriting, because none but Christ was able to satisfy what it required (Heb. 10:9). It took his perfect life and sacrificial death to do this.

v.15. When a Roman emperor won a victory and conquered his foes, he rode through the streets in an open chariot; the captive kings and warriors, stripped of their armour and their hands tied behind their backs in chains, walked before him exposed to public shame and disgrace. Christ has disarmed all the principalities and powers which were against us (Rom. 8:33,34). He has defeated Satan, sin, hell and death. He has made a bold display and public example of them in his cross. We are complete in Christ; he has set the captive free. We are not in bondage to any law, ceremony, or curse.

v.16. Therefore, let no man sit in judgement on you in matters of food and drink or with regard to ceremonies, feast days, or sabbaths. No man can command of us what Christ has not commanded (1 Tim. 4:1-8).

v.17. The Old Testament ceremonies, circumcision, feast days and sacrifices were but shadows or symbols of Christ and his redemptive work. They were in effect only until he came. He is the truth, the body and the substance of all these. To continue in them is to say that Christ, the fulfilment, has not come! (Heb. 10:1-5.)

v.18. Our reward or prize is to win Christ and be found in him, to know him and the power of his resurrected life (Phil. 3:8-14). 'Don't let anyone turn you away from this by insisting on a false humility, self-abasement, worshipping of angels and dead saints, teaching what is not in God's Word (but only in his visions and imagination)'. All false, unscriptural philosophies are products of the flesh and lead away from Christ!

v.19. These men bring reproach upon Christ, who is the only Head of the church. They make angels, the virgin, or other saints to be employed with him as mediators with the Father (1 Tim. 2:5,6). Christ is the *only* Head, Lord, King and Giver of life. The whole body is knit together in him. We receive our life, nourishment, growth and grace only from him! The more we draw from Christ, the more we grow and increase spiritually and the better we will be knit together in love and unity.

v.20.   If we died with Christ by virtue of our union with Christ, if we were buried and rose with him and in him have justification, pardon, redemption and sanctification, if in Christ all the ordinances, ceremonies and types were fulfilled and we are free from these requirements, if in Christ we are redeemed from the curse, covenant and condemnation of the law — why would we want to return to these shadows and types? (Gal. 4:21; 3:10.)

vv.21,22.   'Touch not . . . taste not . . . handle not;' that is, meats, unclean things and other things forbidden by religious rules. These things are of service and reference only to the body; they can be of no value to the soul. They are perishing materials and cease to be when they are not used. The using of them cannot defile, and the abstinence from them cannot sanctify, nor commend us to God. Submission to these ordinances by a believer is not commanded by God, but by false teachers.

v.23.   These religious rules, ceremonies and fleshly practices give the outward appearance of devotion, humility and consecration. All error has something to say in its defence. Men like to serve God with their own inventions. They like to appear to be pious and humble; so they promote self-imposed laws, discipline and punishment of the body; but these are of no value in checking the flesh or sanctifying the heart. They do not honour God, but only indulge natural flesh and its false concept of righteousness (Rom. 10:1-4).

Christ is all

Colossians 3:1-11

v.1.   'If it be true that you are crucified with Christ, buried with him in baptism, risen with him and seated with him in the heavens, then **seek those things which are above**.'

1. Seek the heavenly country (Ps. 17:15; Heb. 11:9,10; 1 Peter 1:3,4).

2. Seek Christ and his righteousness (Phil. 3:9-11).

3. Seek all spiritual blessings, as peace, life and glory (Eph. 1:3; James 1:17; 3:17).

We seek those things which are above; for he is there, seated at God's right hand.

v.2.   '**Set your affection** [your heart] **on things above**.' Unless our hearts are set on the things of Christ, they will not be sought in the proper manner. 'Keep thy heart with all diligence; for out of it are the issues of life' (Prov. 4:23). Do not set your mind, thoughts and desires on the things of this world (Rom. 8:5). Food and clothing, care of families, health and necessities of life are to be sought after and provided for, yet not with anxiety and distress, as if these were our chief end or the source of our chief happiness (Matt. 6:28-34). All the things of this earth shall fade away, 'but he that doeth the will of God abideth for ever' (1 John 2:15-17).

v.3.   As far as this world is concerned (with its riches, honour, temporary glory, fame, pleasures and relationships), '**ye are dead**'! Our new life, our real life and interest, is with Christ in God. '**Hid with Christ**' denotes the secrecy of it (the natural man does not understand it), and the safety of it (it shall never perish). The more we are aware of our union with Christ and the more our minds are set on him, the less interest we have in this world and its passing vanities.

v.4.   Our real glory is yet to come! It will be revealed when
he is revealed in his glory. Christ is our life; his life and ours
are one (Gal. 2:20). He is our hope. He is our happiness; true
happiness is in knowing him. He is our portion; we are joint
heirs with him, and when he comes in his glory, we will enter
into his glory! (1 John 3:1-3; Rom. 8:16-18.)

vv.5,6.   Since we seek things above, are mindful of things
above, are dead to the things of this world and are one with
Christ, we must constantly put to death these sinful desires
that remain in our flesh (Rom. 7:18-23). Let us face our
bodily members and their sinful desires with honesty and truth,
putting them down and refusing to yield to them when they
appear.

Paul lists some of the fleshly temptations which we are to
put down and deaden: fornication, impurity, sensual appetites,
unholy desires and imaginations and all greed and covetousness.
The work of mortification is not perfected in an instant (nor is
it ever completely perfected in this life). So much of this body
of sin and death remains in us that we must make it our daily
task to put down evil thoughts and desires. The Lord's people
are still human and will have a real struggle with the flesh.
However, he will give grace and mercy for every need. The very
fact that we are exhorted to mortify these fleshly appetites
indicates that they still exist to some degree in the believer.
God's wrath is upon the children of disobedience because this
is their way of life.

v.7.   Before we met Christ, this was our way of life. We
walked and lived in these things, giving full release to the flesh,
greed, covetousness and sin. Now we love Christ and long to be
like him in conduct, conversation and attitude. It is not so
much sin in itself that brings the wrath of God, but love for
sin, hardness in sin and continuance in sin. There is sin in his
people, but they confess their sins and he forgives them
(1 John 2:1).

v.8.   Paul returns to his exhortation to put down and mortify
sin in our members. He mentions six sins; the first three are of

the heart and the rest are sins of the mouth! The right order of mortification is to begin with the heart (Matt. 23:26). Proceed then to the tongue and the outward man.

vv. 9, 10. This is regeneration, this is the new birth — the Holy Spirit has created a new man with new desires, new principles, new attitudes. This new man is created in the image of Christ. We know him, his will and his ways. We hate the old man of flesh and continually put him off. By God's grace the new man will grow in grace and the knowledge of Christ until at death the old man will be totally eradicated and we will be like Christ.

v. 11. It is usual for natural men to think that they will be accepted of God because of nationality, ceremony, outward piety, works, or knowledge. It is also usual for men to conclude that God will take less notice of them if they lack these things. This verse clears that up. In regeneration Christ is all (John. 1:12). In righteousness Christ is all (2 Cor. 5:21). In sanctification Christ is all (1 Cor. 1:30). In acceptance Christ is all (Eph. 1:6,7). In love Christ is all (Rom. 8:39). In redemption Christ is all (1 Peter 1:18).

Christian graces

Colossians 3:12-16

In the preceding verses of this chapter the apostle exhorts us to put off the old man with his deeds. The conduct and character of the old man are anger, malice, blasphemy, filthy talk and lies. In these verses we are exhorted as the elect of God, as children of God, to behave as such in thought, word and deed. Put on the new man and his deeds; this is the fruit of the Spirit.

v. 12. It is not sufficient to cease from outward deeds of evil.

We must also learn to do well and live as new creatures in Christ.

'**Put on, as the elect of God**.' There is an inseparable connection between being God's children and behaving like God's children (2 Cor. 5:17; Rom. 8:9; 1 John 4:7,8,20). We do well to question our union with Christ where there is no evidence of growth in the grace of Christ, the love of Christ and the fruit of his Spirit.

'**Bowels of mercy**' — an inward pity and tenderness toward the needs, misery and infirmities of others.

'**Kindness**.' Our sympathy toward others should not only be inward, but outward also, expressed in words, conduct and deeds of kindness.

'**Humbleness of mind**.' This arises from a genuine sense of our own sins, infirmities and short-comings, as well as a sense of God's mercy toward us in Christ (1 Cor. 4:7). We look upon ourselves as the chief of sinners, inferior to others in graces, gifts and knowledge.

'**Meekness**' — the opposite of pride and arrogance. It destroys envy, jealousy and quarrels (1 Peter 3:4). A meek and quiet spirit will lead to patience or long-suffering. We don't feel it necessary to avenge ourselves or even to defend ourselves.

v.13.   As long as we are in the flesh we will have misunderstandings, unpleasantnesses and even injustices (we will feel that our rights have been violated and others have been wrong in what they have said and done). What is to be our attitude? It is to be twofold: 'forbearing' and 'forgiving'. To forbear is to control our emotions, surrendering our rights for the time being in patient hope that God will reveal his purpose and will. To forgive is actually to put the misunderstanding out of mind and restore a state of love and fellowship. This is the way our Lord treats us. He is longsuffering and patient with us, forgiving our sins, remembering them no more!

v.14.   '**Above all things**,' the most necessary grace is love (Matt. 22:36-40; 1 Cor. 13:1-3,13). This is the bond which binds everything together in complete harmony for the glory of God and the good of one another. Knowledge, activity, zeal and morality won't bind us to Christ or to one another.

v.15. Let the peace which comes through Christ (Rom. 5:1) and the peace which comes from Christ (Rom. 12:18; 14:19; 2 Cor. 13:11,12) actually rule our hearts, deciding and settling all matters that arise in our minds or in the assembly. As members of the body of Christ we were called to live in peace and love (1 Cor. 7:15). Let us be thankful and appreciative, first to God for all grace and then to one another. These virtues are absolutely necessary. Where love, peace and thanksgiving are absent, faith is absent!

v.16. We are exhorted to a diligent study of God's Word. This is not for information and doctrine alone, but that God's Word might become such a part of us that it is said to dwell in us as a member of the family lives in a home. It is loved, respected, obeyed and delighted in richly (Ps. 1:1,2) in an abundant fashion. We are not to study just one part of the Scripture, but all of it, that we may benefit and grow in grace (1 Peter 2:1,2). It is not only the duty of the ministers to teach, encourage and instruct others; but it is the duty of all believers to witness, teach and encourage one another in spiritual matters. This can be done in private, in groups and in public worship. It is all to be done as unto the Lord, for the glory of the Lord and from the heart.

The common rule for all our actions

Colossians 3:17-25

v.17. This is the key verse in our study. Paul gives us a common rule for all our actions in worship and in daily life. They are to be done in the name of our Lord Jesus Christ, for his glory and with thanksgiving to the Father for our interest in Christ, our position in Christ and our acceptance in Christ.

1. Whether in preaching, singing, praying, teaching, or in conversation with other believers, let us do what we do in the name of Christ and for his glory.

2. Whether in the home, on the job, or in any of our business and social contacts, we are not left at liberty to do as we please, but we are to aim at his glory and his will.

3. This will bring God's blessings, will bring unity of heart and purpose, will drive out divisions and strife, if we do all that we do, not for selfish purposes, but for Christ's sake.

vv.18,19.   From this verse to the end of the chapter, Paul talks about the duties and deeds which relate to Christians as they are members of a family. In this family there are three pairs: husbands and wives, parents and children and masters and servants. He points out the duties of each to the other, to be fulfilled for the glory of Christ and in the name of Christ.

In order for a home to be well-ordered, a place of love and contentment and for Christ to have pre-eminence, these two things must be true:

1. The wife must be in subjection to the husband as is fit in the Lord, obeying him, respecting his judgements and decisions, and following his leadership as long as he does not violate the Word of God (Eph. 5:22-24; Gen. 3:16).

2. The husband should love his wife, treat her with kindness, respect and defend her before his parents, children and all who would discredit or abuse her. Husband and wife are one in the Lord and must not suffer this union to be broken, either in their own eyes or the eyes of others, particularly their children. No home can be built for Christ's glory or for our good if we are pulling our separate, selfish ways. We walk together in love and affection if we seek the glory of Christ.

vv.20,21.   Do you children want to be happy? Do you want God's blessings on your lives? Do you desire to live for the glory of God and do all things in the name of Christ? Then 'Obey your parents'. Honour your father and mother. Respect them and their decisions. Speak respectfully of and to them. This is well pleasing to the Lord! (Exod. 20:12.)

Parents, do not abuse your parental authority. There are

two dangerous directions we take in raising children: either being too hard and unreasonable with them, or being too indulgent and easy with them. Either way children will become discouraged, spoiled and rebellious. If we can seek God's will and not our own, God's glory and not our own, God's tenderness and way and not our own in dealing with our children, we will build a relationship the Lord will bless.

v.22. 'Servants' here refers to all who work in the employ or service of someone else:

1. Let us give an honest, dedicated, full effort in our labours as if we were working for the Lord, not just in appearance, but with a dedicated heart.

2. Let us be concerned for our employer's business, property and profit, not stealing, wasting, or misusing equipment or tools.

3. Let us be content with our pay, asking for it in the right spirit, considering his ability to pay.

'Masters,' you have some obligations to your servants:

1. Give them fair and equal pay. They have families to support, children to educate and they enjoy the same things you enjoy.

2. Expect them to work, produce and promote the business; but don't be unreasonable. Treat them as you want to be treated. Don't lay burdens on them you are unwilling to bear.

3. Treat them with respect. A man may dress poorly or have less ability and education, but he is a son of God. He is an important person in the eyes of God.

vv.23-25. 'Whatever you do in all these areas (husbands and wives, children and parents, servants and masters), do what you do sincerely, with all your heart, as unto the Lord and before the Lord.' If we are his children, our activities have a higher purpose and calling than just building relationships and programmes that will one day crumble. We are serving the Lord Jesus Christ and his greater glory. From him we shall receive a 'well done' or judgement.

Speaking to God and to men

Colossians 4:1-18

v.1.   This verse belongs to the preceding chapter (it has no
connection with what follows). The apostle, having exhorted
servants to a proper discharge of their duties (as unto the
Lord), proceeds to instruct those who hire and work servants
to treat them in a just and equal manner. 'Treat them with
respect, encouraging them in their work, and giving them fair
wages. Remember that you have a Master in heaven' (Matt.
6:15; 18:23-35).

v.2.   There are three important things mentioned here in
regard to our prayers.
   1. **'Continue in prayer.'** This does not mean that we should
pray all the time. That would be impossible. We can and ought
to live in an attitude of prayer and fellowship with God. This
does mean to pray frequently about all things. A day should
not pass without prayer.
   2. **'Watch** in prayer.' Be alert and intent in prayer. This is
said in opposition to cold, formal and careless praying (which
God despises). When we pray, let it be an undivided, sincere
communion with the living God.
   3. **'With thanksgiving'** (Phil. 4:6). A believer always has
mercies for which to be thankful. How shall we succeed in our
present request if we are not thankful for what has gone
before?

vv.3,4.   Paul requests prayer for himself and others who
minister the Word.
   1. 'Pray that a door of opportunity may be opened' (1 Cor.
16:9; 2 Cor. 2:12).
   2. 'Pray that the door of men's hearts may be opened.' Men
may hear the gospel with natural ears and still not hear with

the heart (1 Cor. 2:9,10). The gospel of God's grace and glory is a mystery which must be revealed by the power of God's Spirit, else men remain in darkness even after hearing (Matt. 13:10-13; Gal. 1:15; 1 Cor. 2:14).

3. 'Pray that the door of my lips may be opened. Pray that God will give me the words to say, the ability to say them, and the wisdom to do it for his glory! Pray that I may preach the gospel faithfully, boldly, with clearness of speech as I ought (Matt. 9:37,38).

v.5.   **'Them that are without'** are unbelievers, people who are not members of the church family. The church is the household of faith; those who are unbelievers are not of this household. It becomes us in our communication with these people to behave wisely and in such a manner that the gospel is not blasphemed and reproached. Do all that you can in your contact with unbelievers to gain their respect, affection and approval of your conduct, conversation and attitude. We should be known in our families, our community and our business circles as peaceful, honest, holy and kind people.

v.6.   **'Let your speech be always with grace.'** This is not just to talk about the grace of God, but our speech should reveal the grace of God.

1. Speak the truth faithfully and sincerely, without lying, flattery, or exaggeration.

2. Speak in love, avoiding gossip, whisperings, or anything that is injurious to the character of another. Avoid sowing discord or division.

3. Speak kindly and pleasantly. Hard words reveal a hard heart. Unkind, cutting remarks reveal a bitter spirit.

Grace is to the speech what salt is to meat. It makes it acceptable, good to the ear and a blessing to the heart. Grace in the heart will teach you how you ought to answer any person. Knowledge is not acquired by speaking, but it ought to go before it!

vv.7,8.   Paul was in prison in Rome. He sent Tychicus and Onesimus to declare his state to the Colossian believers, to inform them of what was done in Rome, and that these ministers might comfort and encourage them. The rest of the epistle is to encourage specifically certain persons in the church.